EASY PIANO SELECTIONS

ANDREW LLOYD WEBBER'S

TM © 2021 The Really Useful Group Limited

The musical works contained in this edition may not be publicly performed in a dramatic form or context except under license from The Really Useful Group Limited, 6 Catherine Street, London WC2B 5JY

For more information please visit **www.andrewlloydwebber.com**

Andrew Lloyd Webber™ is a trade mark owned by Andrew Lloyd Webber.

ISBN 978-1-70514-159-5

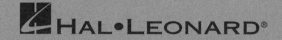

Visit Hal Leonard Online at
www.halleonard.com

Contact us:
Hal Leonard
7777 West Bluemound Road
Milwaukee, WI 53213
Email: info@halleonard.com

In Europe, contact:
Hal Leonard Europe Limited
42 Wigmore Street
Marylebone, London, W1U 2RN
Email: info@halleonardeurope.com

In Australia, contact:
Hal Leonard Australia Pty. Ltd.
4 Lentara Court
Cheltenham, Victoria, 3192 Australia
Email: info@halleonard.com.au

CONTENTS

4   BAD CINDERELLA

8   SO LONG

16   UNBREAKABLE

24   MAN'S MAN

19   ONLY YOU, LONELY YOU

32   I KNOW YOU

48   BEAUTY HAS A PRICE

39   THE CINDERELLA WALTZ

65   I KNOW I HAVE A HEART

70   I AM NO LONGER ME

58   MOMENT OF TRIUMPH

90   FAR TOO LATE

76   THE WEDDING MARCH

80   THE VANQUISHING OF THE THREE-HEADED SEA WITCH

BAD CINDERELLA

Music by ANDREW LLOYD WEBBER
Lyrics by DAVID ZIPPEL
Book by EMERALD FENNELL

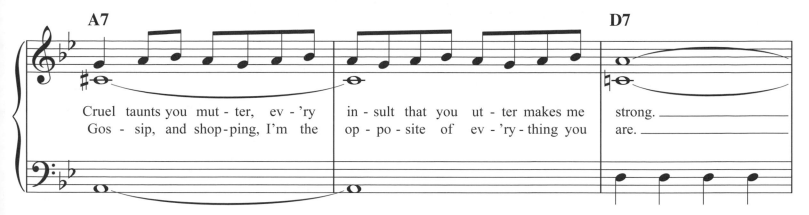

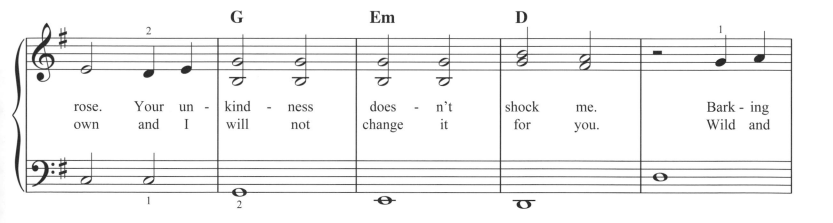

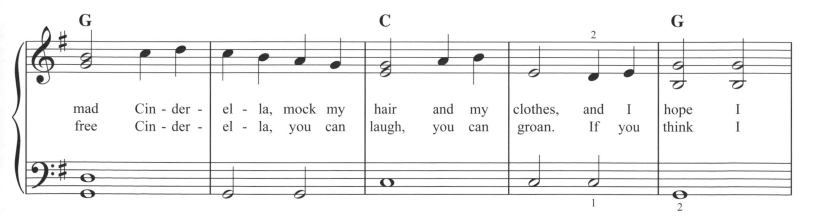

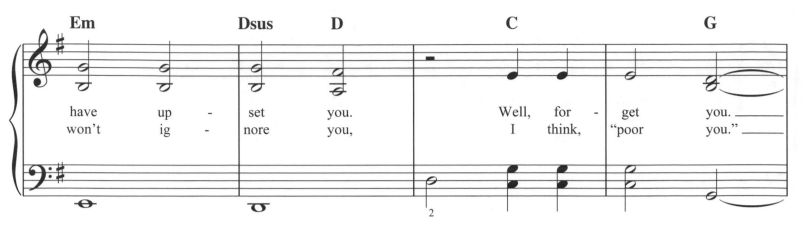

have up - set you.
won't ig - nore you,
Well, for - get you.
I think, "poor you."

They call me a wretch, a witch, ___ well, choose one.

Ev - 'ry fair - y tale, for sure, ___ can use one. Sor - ry I'm so rude, sor - ry

you're so lame. I won't play your game. ___ Call me

bad Cin - der - el - la, I take pride when you sneer. I am
bad Cin - der - el - la, I will not say good - bye. You've been

proud that I'm not like you. I - ron - clad Cin - der -
hate - ful since I met you. Bark - ing mad Cin - der -

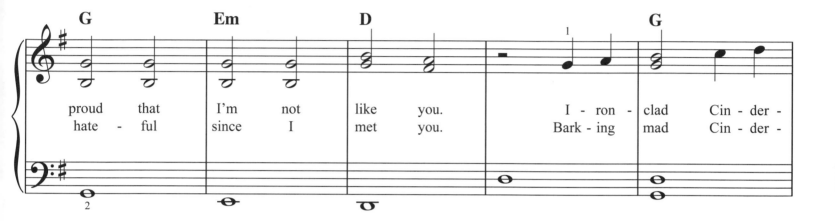

el - la, I face life with no fear and a more than sky - high
el - la, fly - ing high in the sky, and I hope I have up -

I. - Q. Yes, I'm
set you. Well, for - get you!
poco rit.

SO LONG

Music by ANDREW LLOYD WEBBER
Lyrics by DAVID ZIPPEL
Book by EMERALD FENNELL

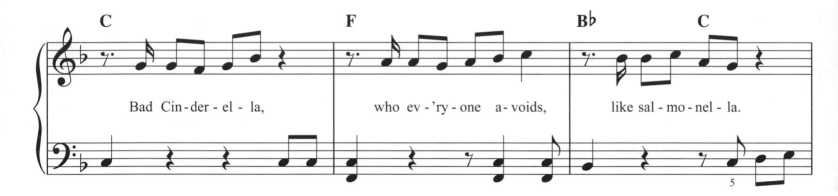

So long, my freak-y friend, Bad Cin-der-el-la, who ev-'ry-one a-voids, like sal-mo-nel-la.

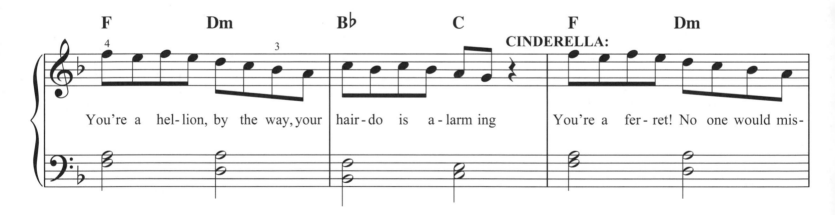

You're a hel-lion, by the way, your hair-do is a-larm ing You're a fer-ret! No one would mis-

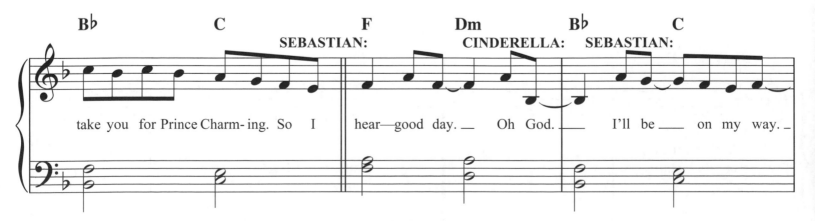

take you for Prince Charm-ing. So I hear—good day.— Oh God.— I'll be— on my way.—

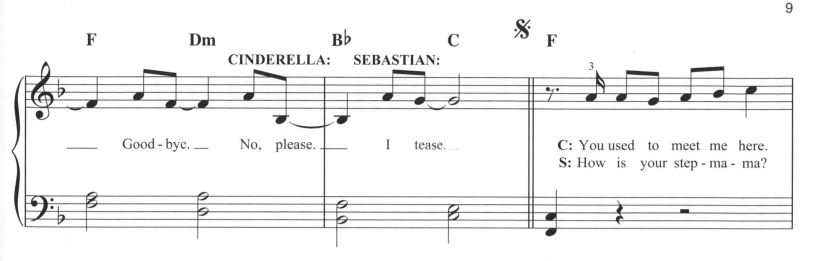

CINDERELLA: SEBASTIAN:

Good - bye. __ No, please. __ I tease. __   C: You used to meet me here.
S: How is your step - ma - ma?

You nev - er show up.   S: Now that I'm next in line   I've had to grow up.
C: She lives to goad me,   while dream - ing of the day   she can un - load me.

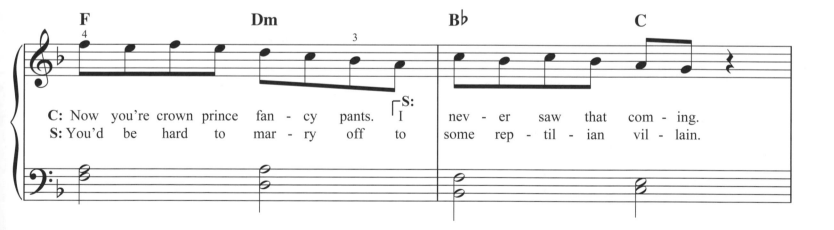

C: Now you're crown prince fan - cy pants.   S: I nev - er saw that com - ing.
S: You'd be hard to mar - ry off to   some rep - til - ian vil - lain.

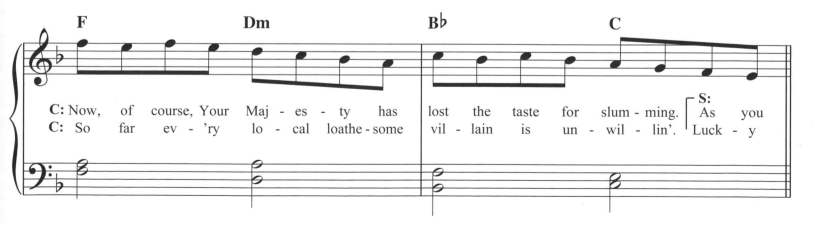

C: Now, of course, Your Maj - es - ty has   lost the taste for slum - ming.   S: As you
C: So far ev - 'ry lo - cal loathe - some   vil - lain is un - wil - lin'.   Luck - y

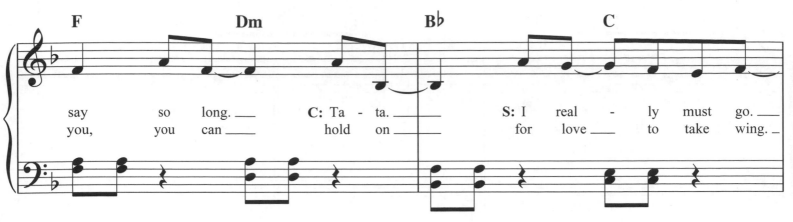

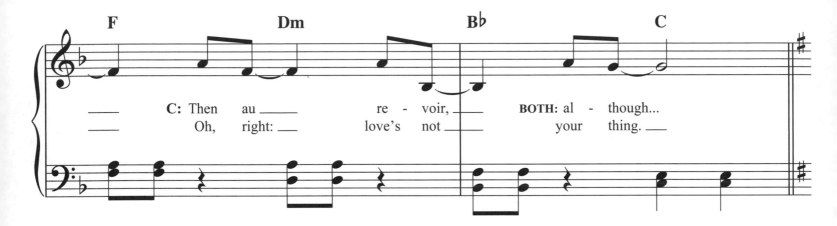

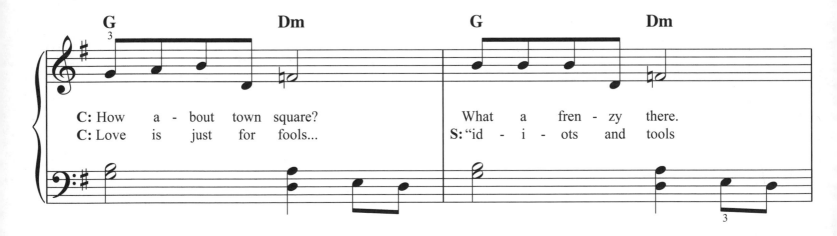

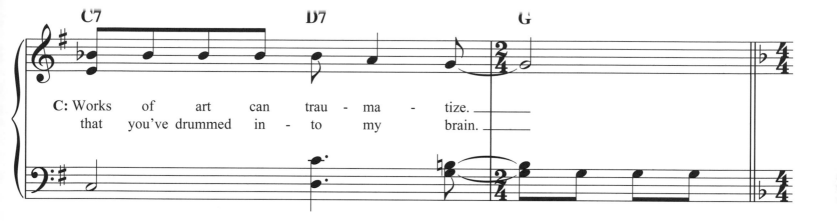

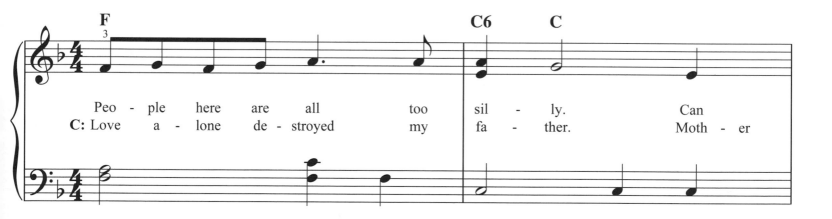

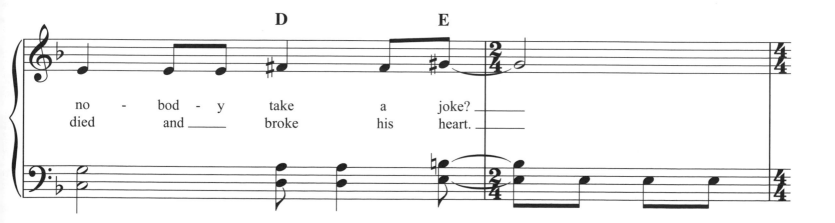

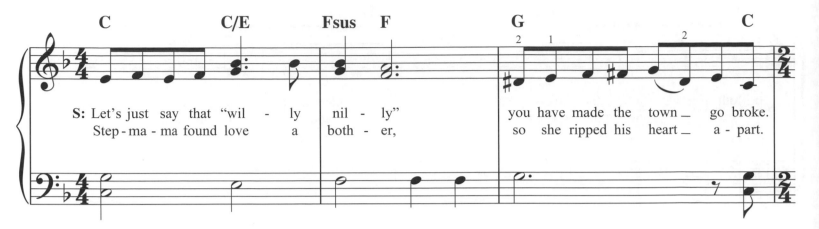

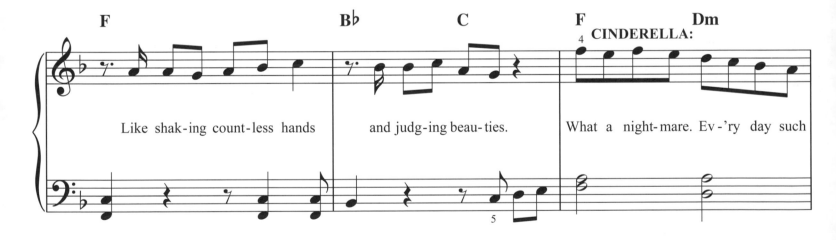

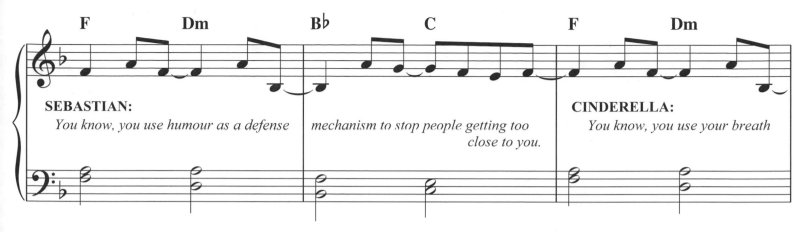

SEBASTIAN:
You know, you use humour as a defense | *mechanism to stop people getting too close to you.*

CINDERELLA:
You know, you use your breath

D.S. al Coda

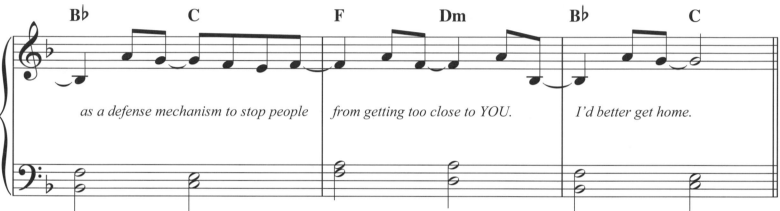

as a defense mechanism to stop people | *from getting too close to YOU.* | *I'd better get home.*

CODA

N.C.

SEBASTIAN:

I think I'd bet-ter go. | I've o-ver-stayed here.

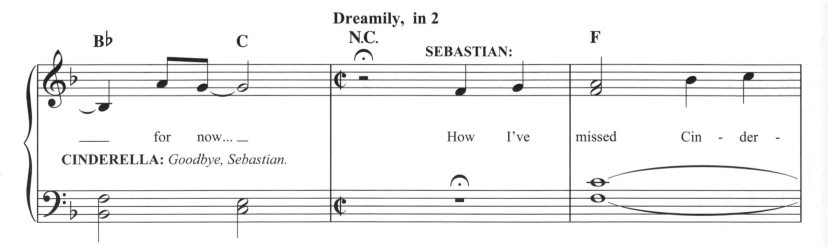

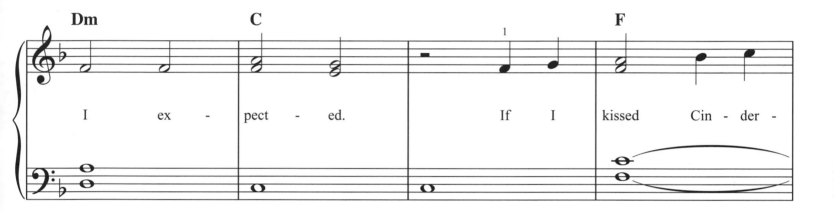

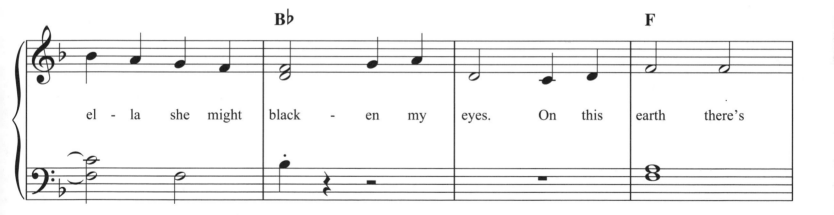

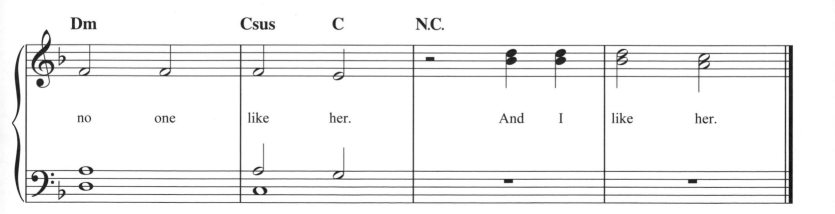

UNBREAKABLE

Music by ANDREW LLOYD WEBBER
Lyrics by DAVID ZIPPEL
Book by EMERALD FENNELL

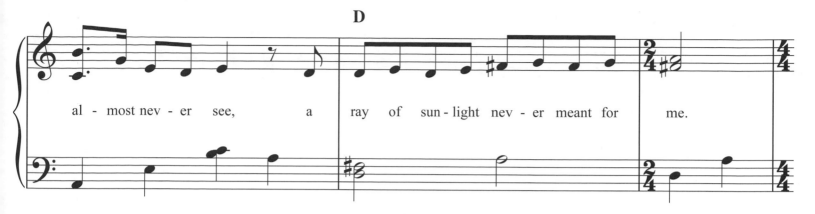

al-most nev-er see, a ray of sun-light nev-er meant for me.

What was I think-ing? Hard as a dia-mond, trapped in a coal mine,

I'm just a girl who is bur-ied a-live. I have a tem-per, I can't con-trol mine.

Am I un-break-a-ble? Will I sur-vive? But my friend, no, the prince, once was

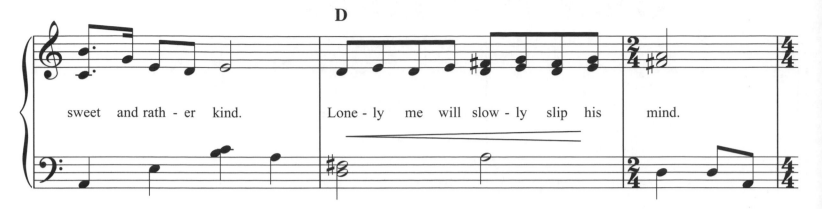

sweet and rath - er kind. Lone - ly me will slow - ly slip his mind.

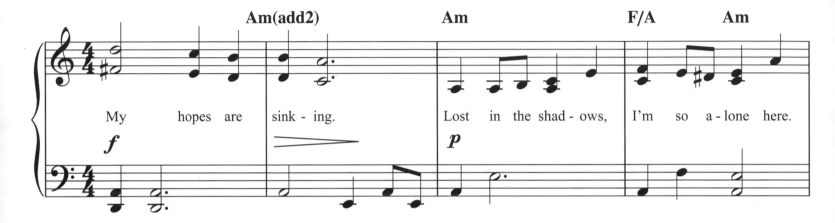

My hopes are sink - ing. Lost in the shad - ows, I'm so a - lone here.

f *p*

Just hold-ing on till the day I can go. Hard - ship and cruel - ty's all that I've known here.

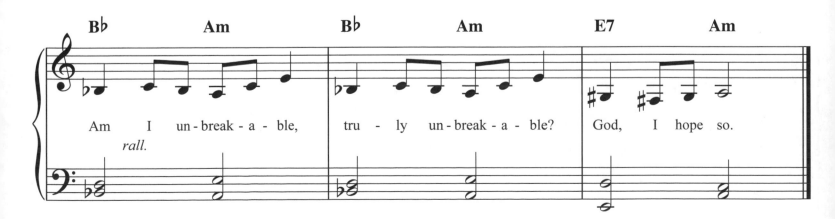

Am I un - break - a - ble, tru - ly un - break - a - ble? God, I hope so.

rall.

ONLY YOU, LONELY YOU

Music by ANDREW LLOYD WEBBER
Lyrics by DAVID ZIPPEL
Book by EMERALD FENNELL

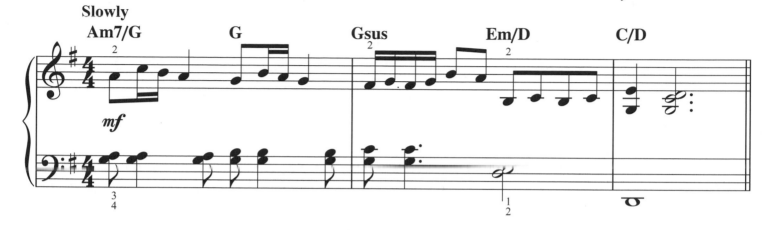

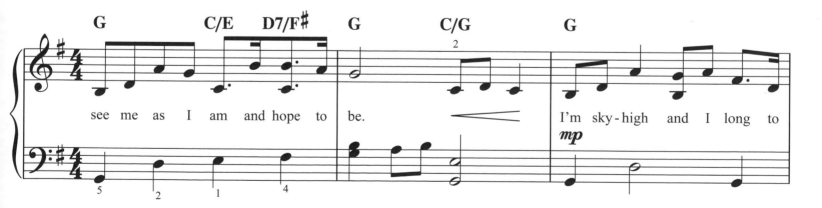

show you. My whole world is al-tered yet I don't say a thing. On-ly

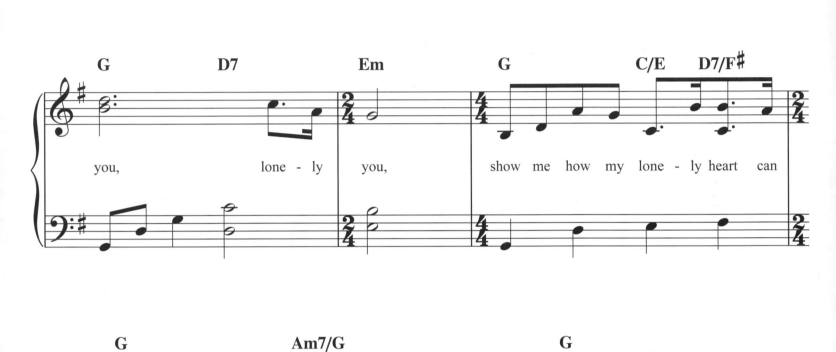

you, lone-ly you, show me how my lone-ly heart can

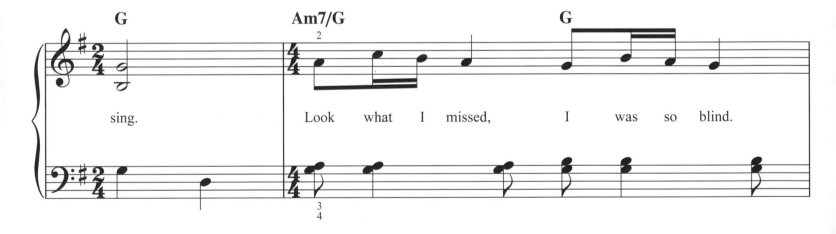

sing. Look what I missed, I was so blind.

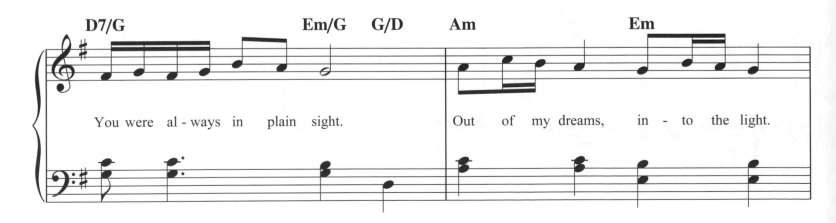

You were al-ways in plain sight. Out of my dreams, in-to the light.

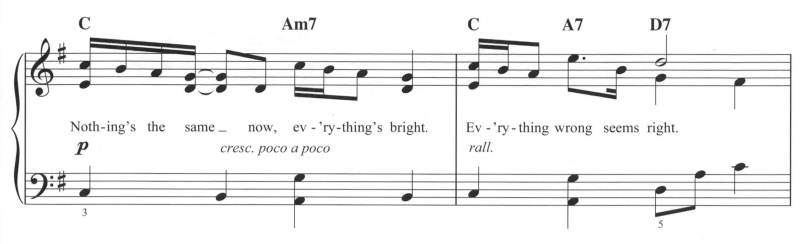

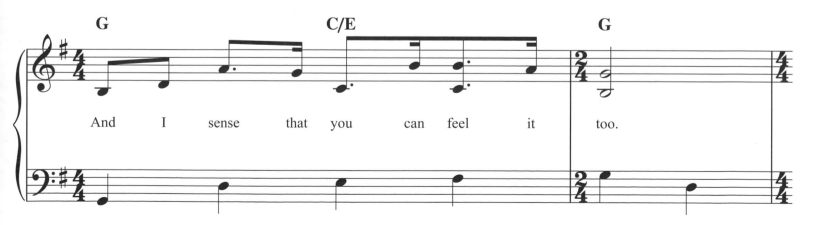

Why don't I speak, say it out loud, tell you how I real - ly feel?

You were right there, five feet a - way. Why was I tongue - tied, ev - er so dull?

cresc. poco a poco

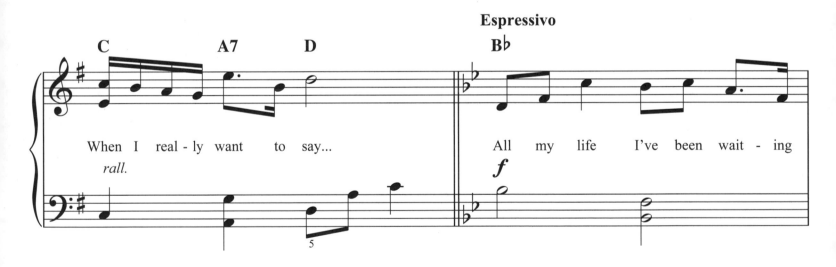

When I real - ly want to say... All my life I've been wait - ing

rall.

for you. You were born to change my life but

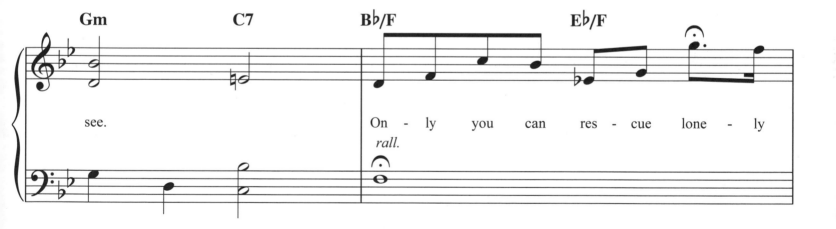

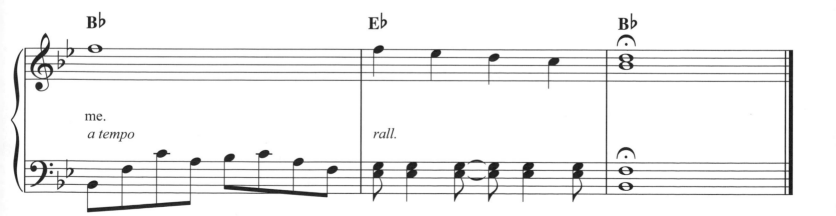

MAN'S MAN

Music by ANDREW LLOYD WEBBER
Lyrics by DAVID ZIPPEL
Book by EMERALD FENNELL

Moderately, freely

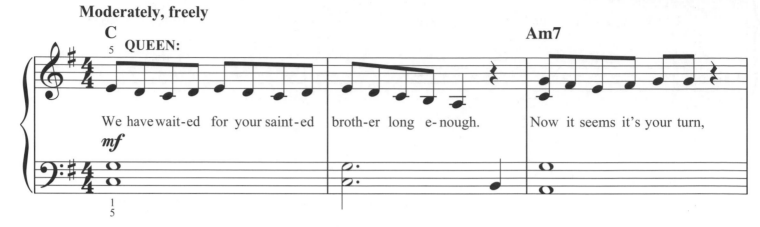

Moderate March, steadily

Mark my word: there's no one be-fore or since who is the e-qual of our sweet prince. True! What a

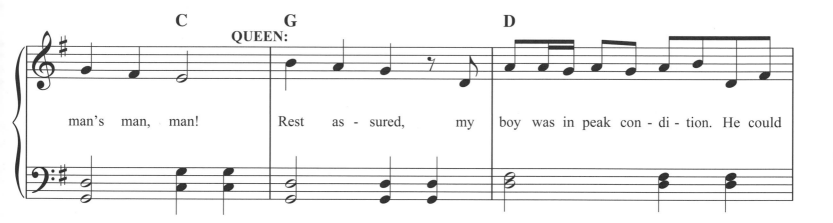

man's man, man! Rest as-sured, my boy was in peak con-di-tion. He could

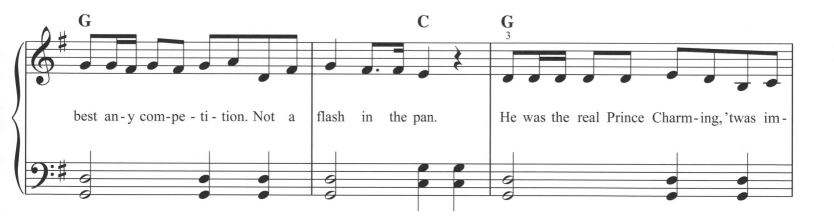

best an-y com-pe-ti-tion. Not a flash in the pan. He was the real Prince Charm-ing, 'twas im-

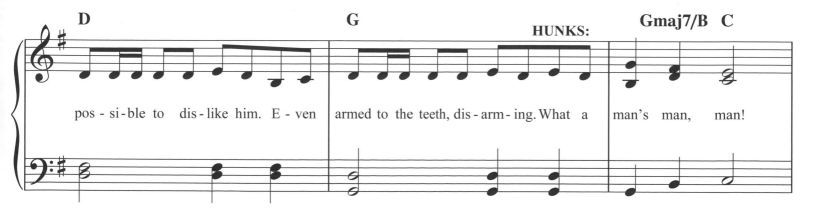

pos-si-ble to dis-like him. E-ven armed to the teeth, dis-arm-ing. What a man's man, man!

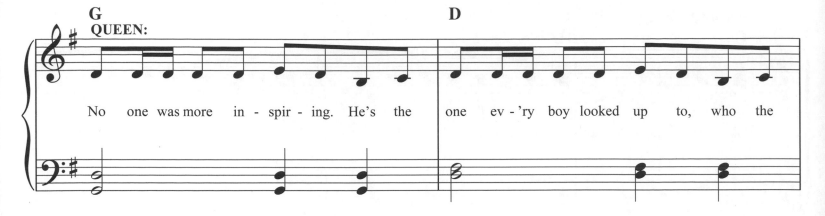

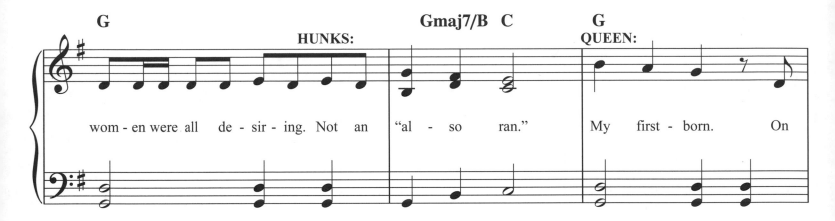

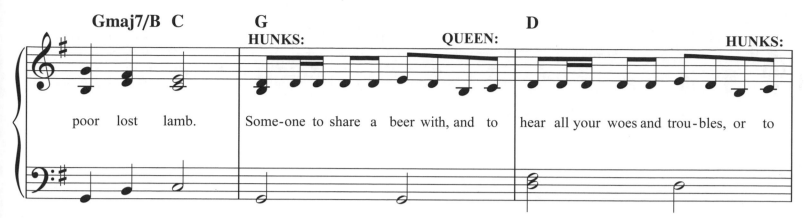

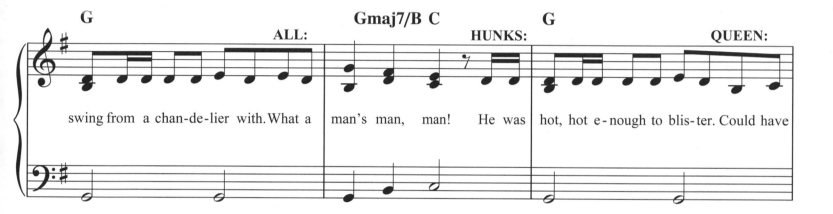

man's man, man! Off the chart, so hand-some, but not a vain male. He looked

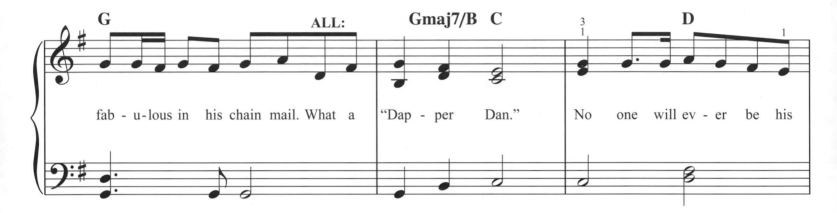

fab-u-lous in his chain mail. What a "Dap-per Dan." No one will ev-er be his

e-qual. Lord knows, his broth-er's not the se-quel. He was

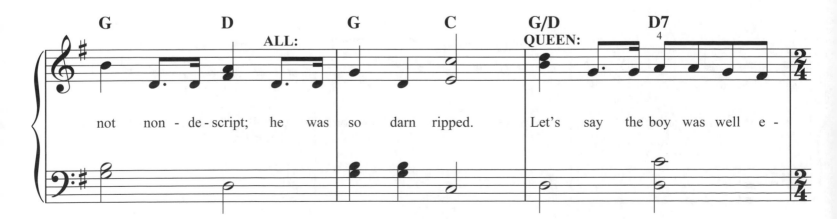

not non-de-script; he was so darn ripped. Let's say the boy was well e-

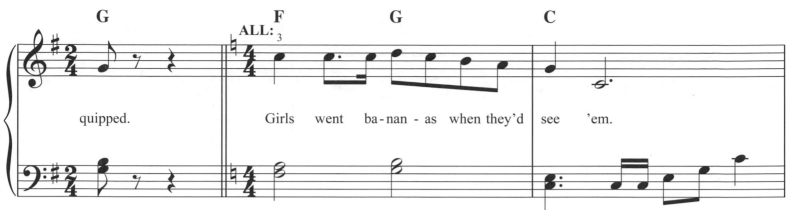

quipped. Girls went ba-nan-as when they'd see 'em.

Buns that be-long in a mu - se - um. And we must make it clear, he was

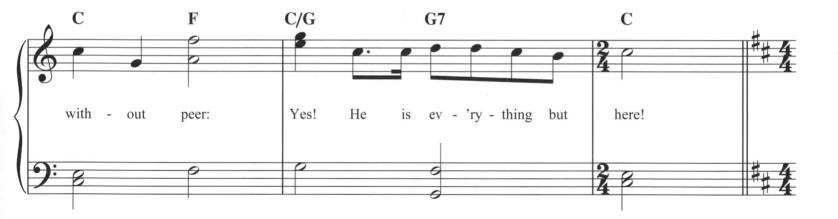

with - out peer: Yes! He is ev - 'ry - thing but here!

Slowly

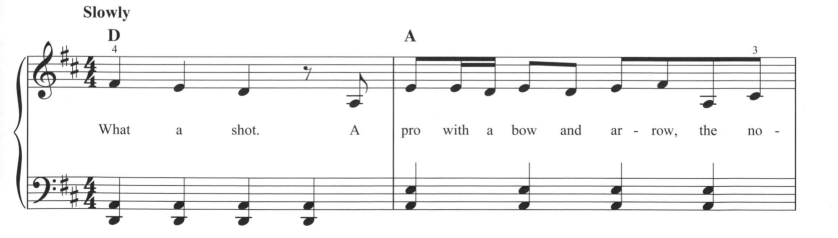

What a shot. A pro with a bow and ar - row, the no -

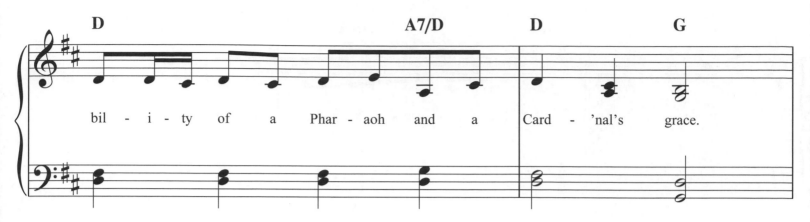

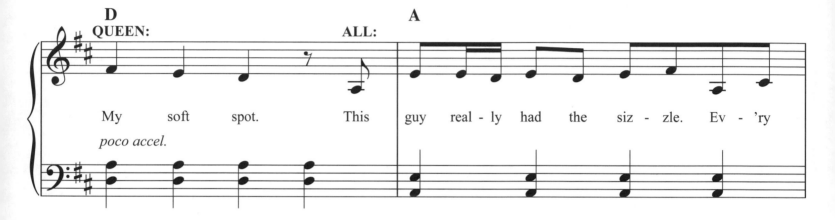

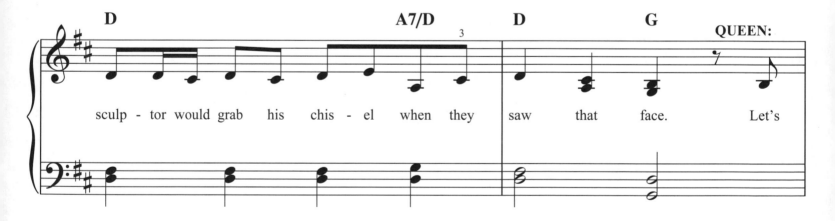

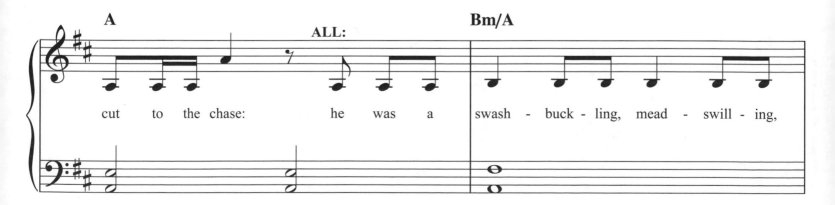

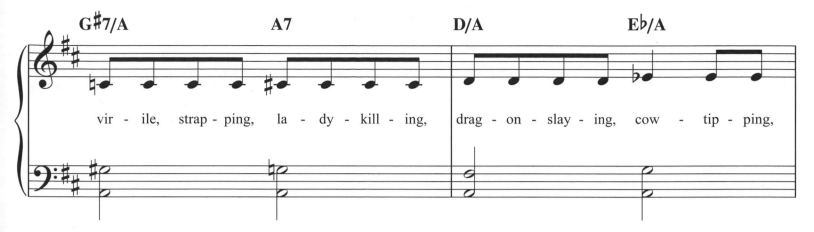

virile, strap-ping, la-dy-kill-ing, drag-on-slay-ing, cow-tip-ping,

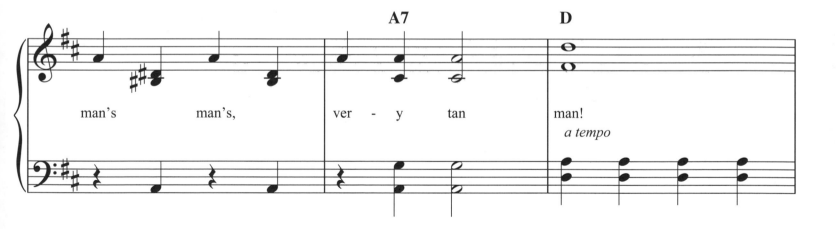

li-on-heart-ed, bod-ice-rip-ping, knuck-le-drag-ging, prin-cess-shag-ging,

rall.

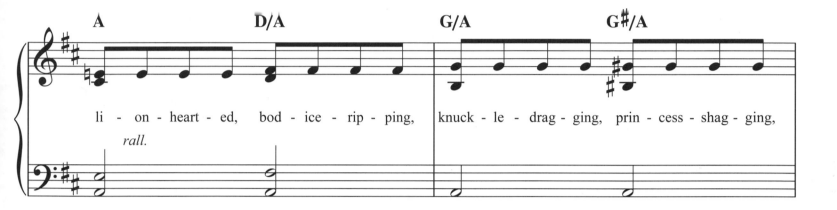

man's man's, ver-y tan man!

a tempo

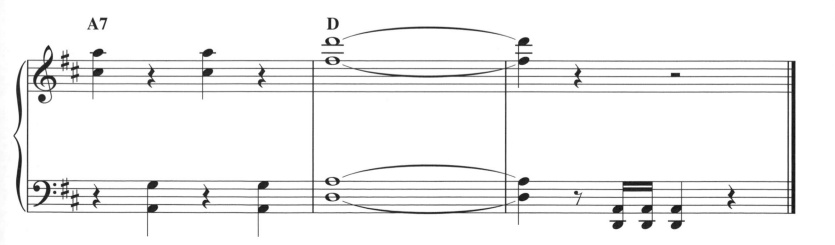

I KNOW YOU

Music by ANDREW LLOYD WEBBER
Lyrics by DAVID ZIPPEL
Book by EMERALD FENNELL

Easy Waltz

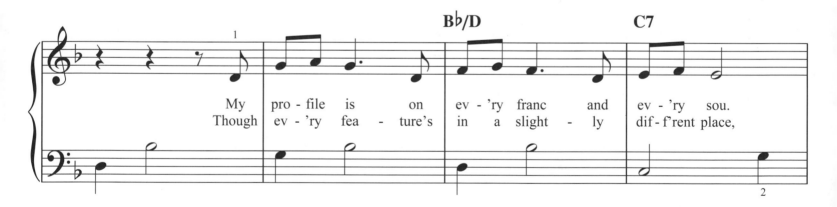

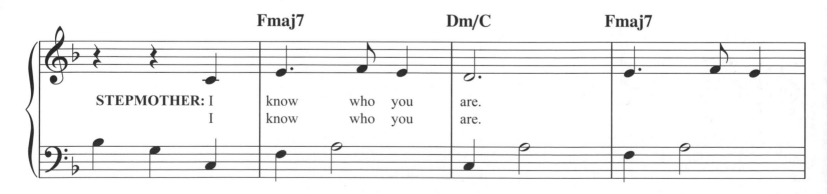

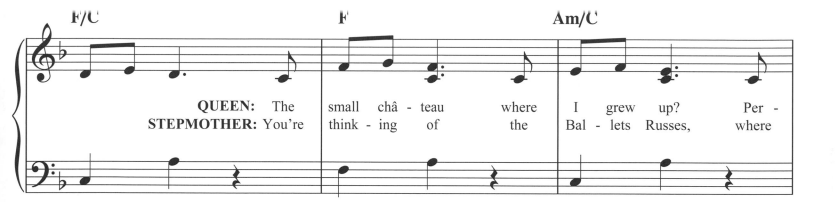

are.
are.

But why
But why

mf

dredge   up   old
poke through your

mem - o - ries,
chif - fe - robe?

times   you got
One   nev - er

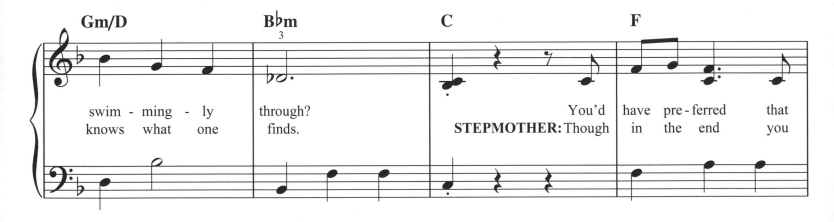

swim - ming - ly
knows what one

through?
finds.

You'd have pre - ferred   that
STEPMOTHER: Though in the end   you

I had nev - er
may dig up   a

breathed a word.
use - ful friend.

I
Two

Am/C   **Fmaj7**   **Gm(add4)**   **C7**

know   you.   I   know
like   minds.   I   know

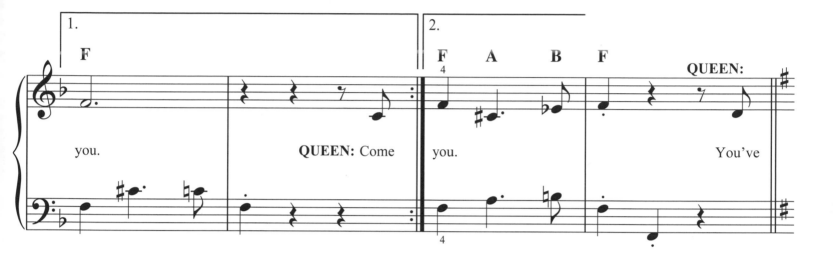

1.   **2.**

F   **F**   **A**   **B**   **F**   **QUEEN:**

you.   **QUEEN:** Come   you.   You've

G   **Bm/D**   **Em/G**

quite a knack   for   bring - ing back   old   mem - o - ries.

G/D   **STEPMOTHER:**   **G**   **Bm/D**

To   help you, dear,   to   see the for - est

for the trees.   Now I re-call you

dressed in tights,   on a tra-peze?   I know who you

are.   An-oth-er time, an-

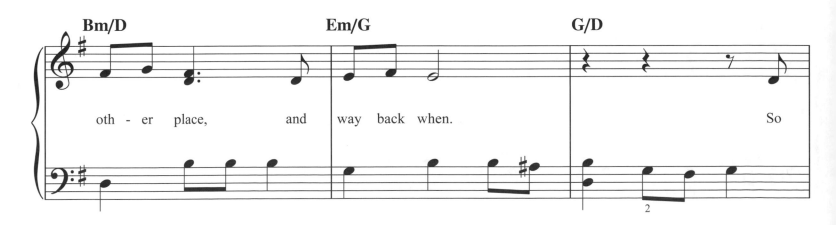

oth-er place,   and way back when.   So

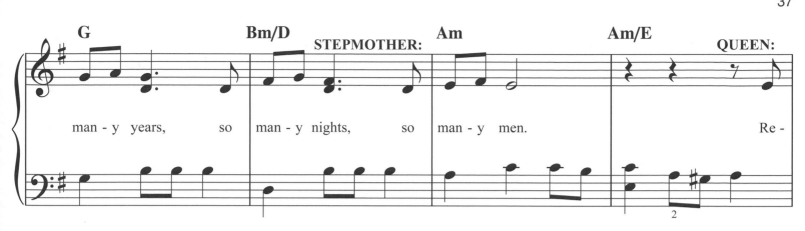

G   Bm/D   **STEPMOTHER:** Am   Am/E   **QUEEN:**

man - y years, so man - y nights, so man - y men.   Re -

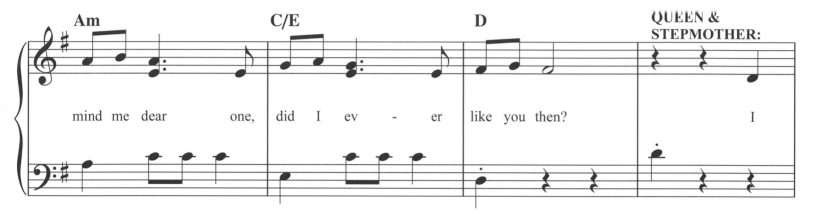

Am   C/E   D   **QUEEN &**
STEPMOTHER:

mind me dear one, did I ev - er like you then?   I

Gmaj7   Em/D   G+   G/D

know who you are.

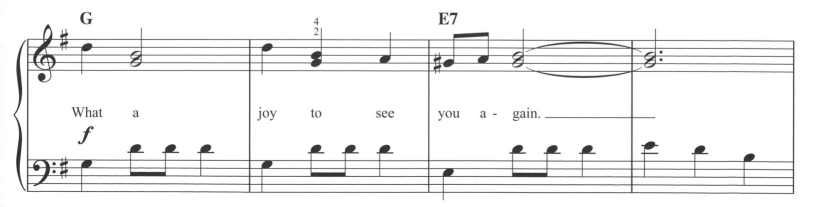

G   E7

What a joy to see you a - gain.

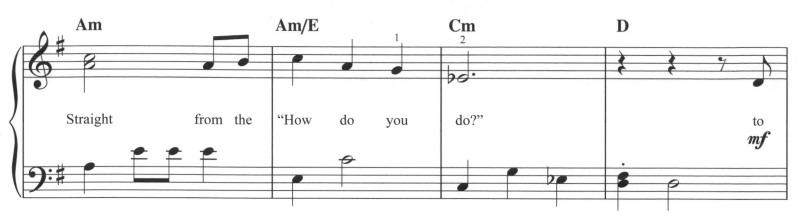

Am   Am/E   Cm   D

Straight from the "How do you do?" to

G   Bm/D   E7

in the end dis - cov - er - ing a long - lost friend. _____

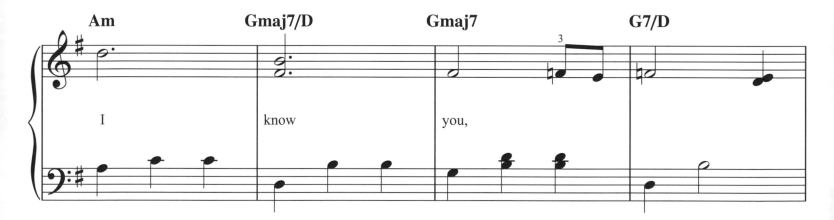

Am   Gmaj7/D   Gmaj7   G7/D

I   know   you,

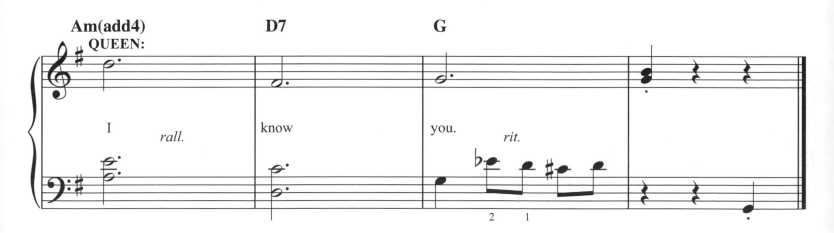

Am(add4)   D7   G
QUEEN:

I   *rall.*   know   you.   *rit.*

THE CINDERELLA WALTZ

Music by ANDREW LLOYD WEBBER
Lyrics by DAVID ZIPPEL
Book by EMERALD FENNELL

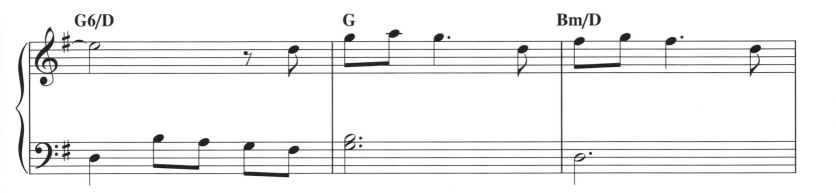

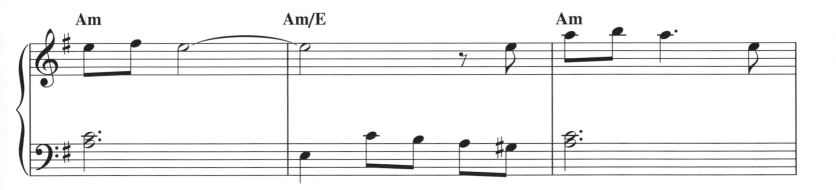

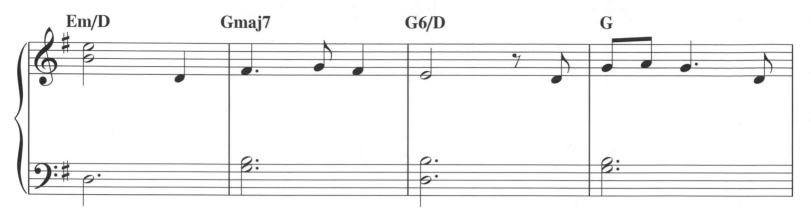

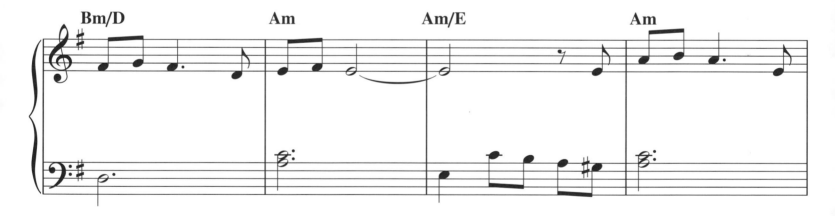

42

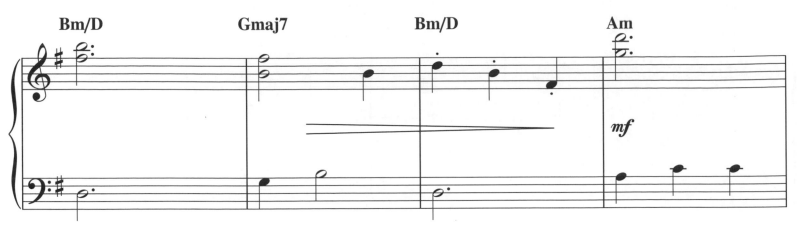

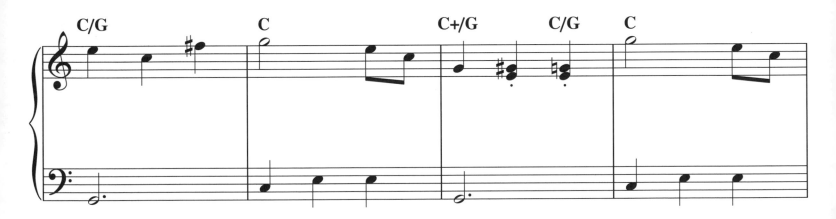

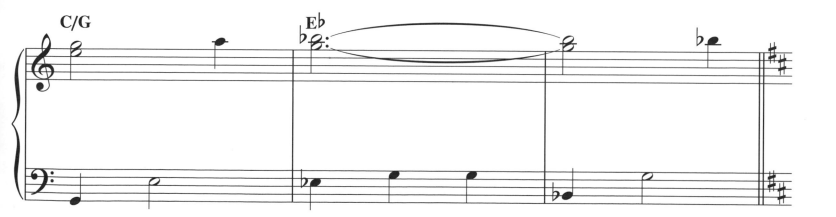

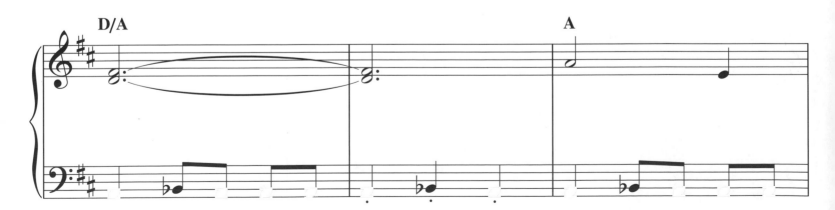

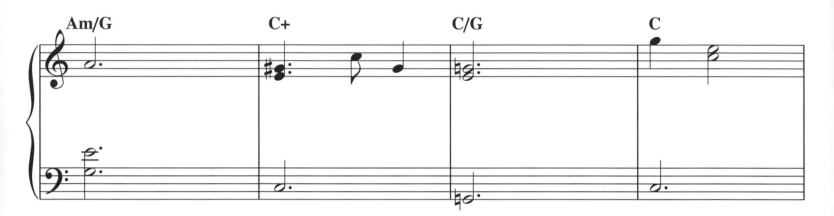

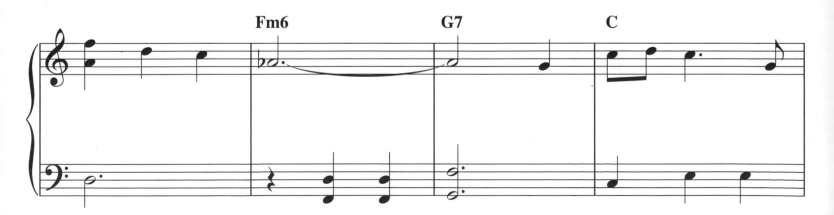

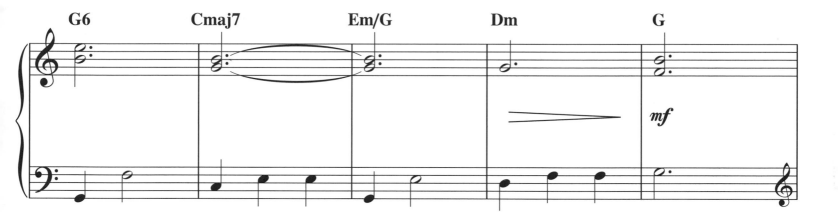

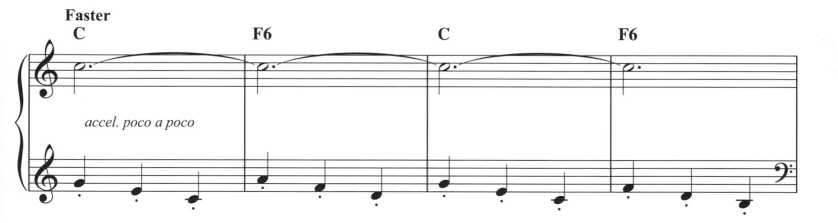

BEAUTY HAS A PRICE

Music by ANDREW LLOYD WEBBER
Lyrics by DAVID ZIPPEL
Book by EMERALD FENNELL

Moderately

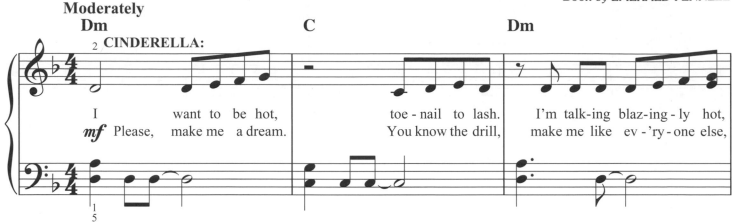

CINDERELLA:

I want to be hot,
Please, make me a dream.

toe - nail to lash.
You know the drill,

I'm talk-ing blaz-ing-ly hot,
make me like ev-'ry-one else,

I mean like vol-can-ic ash.
on-ly a lot bet-ter still.

I wan-na set men on fire
Just like that god-dess from Greece,

and make them wild with de - sire.
you know, who launched all the ships.

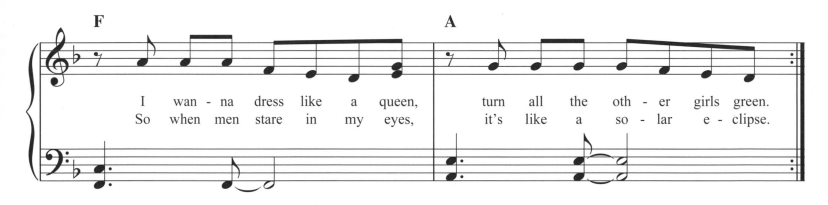

I wan - na dress like a queen,
So when men stare in my eyes,

turn all the oth - er girls green.
it's like a so - lar e - clipse.

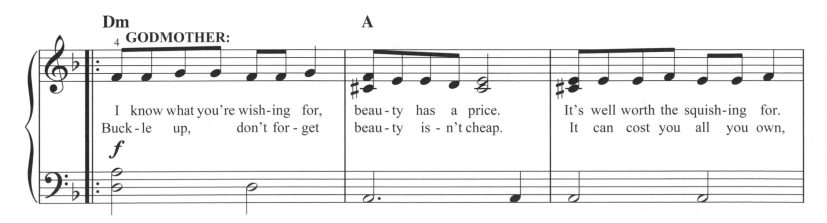

GODMOTHER:

I know what you're wish-ing for,
Buck-le up, don't for - get

beau - ty has a price.
beau - ty is - n't cheap.

It's well worth the squish-ing for.
It can cost you all you own,

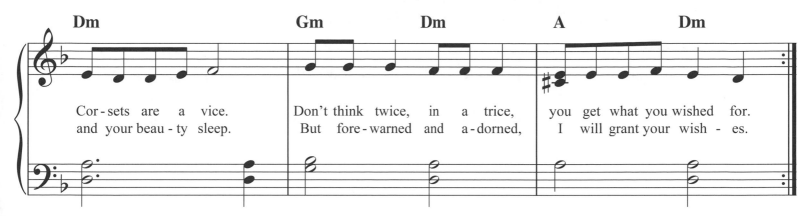

Cor-sets are a vice.
and your beau-ty sleep.
Don't think twice, in a trice,
But fore-warned and a-dorned,
you get what you wished for.
I will grant your wish - es.

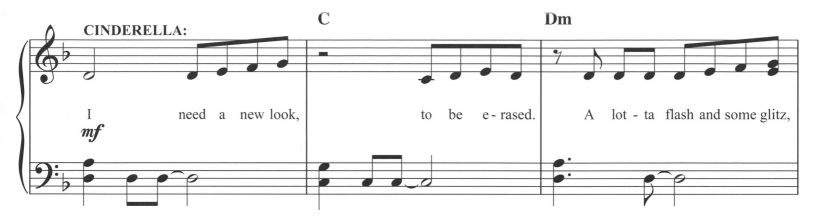

CINDERELLA:

I need a new look, to be e-rased. A lot-ta flash and some glitz,

with just a smid-geon of taste. A sex-y blonde or bru-nette, some-one that I've nev-er met.

GODMOTHER:

Let's go for way O. T. T., I wan-na dis-ap-pear me. I can take care of this,

let me first ex - plain. Get a met - a - mor - pho - sis, beau - ty e - quals pain.

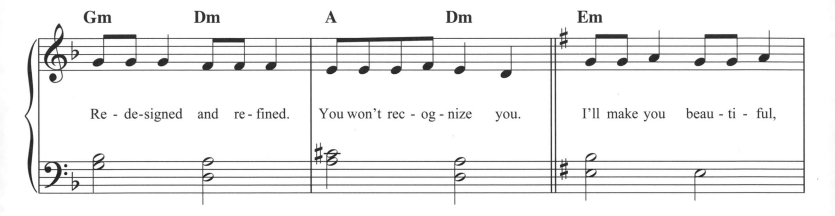

Re - de-signed and re - fined. You won't rec - og - nize you. I'll make you beau - ti - ful,

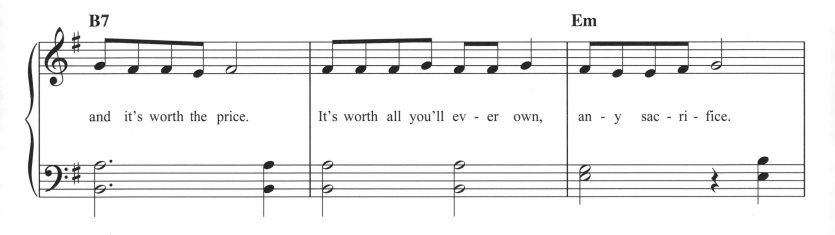

and it's worth the price. It's worth all you'll ev - er own, an - y sac - ri - fice.

So my child, let's go wild, you shall go with bells on. There is no mag - ic, it's

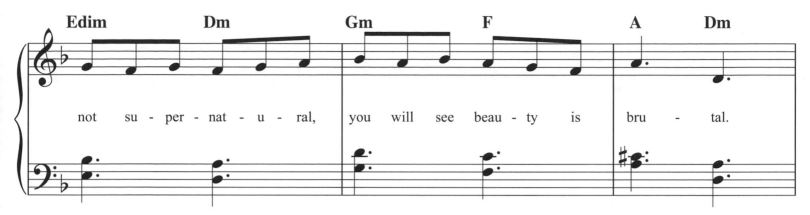

not su - per - nat - u - ral, you will see beau - ty is bru - tal.

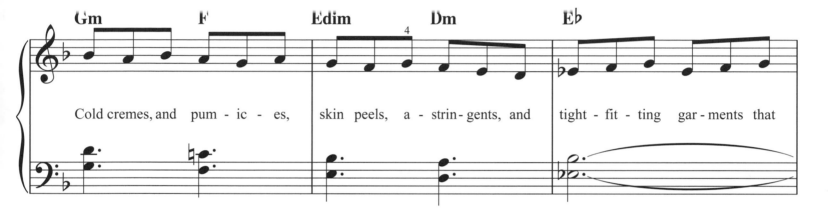

Cold cremes, and pum - ic - es, skin peels, a - strin - gents, and tight - fit - ting gar - ments that

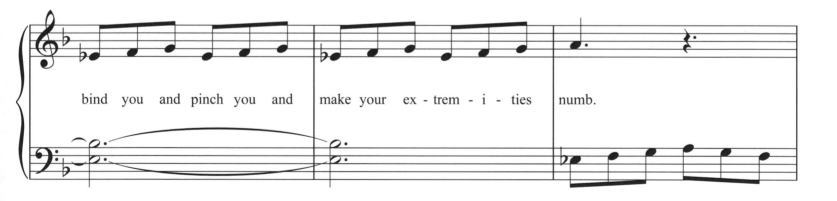

bind you and pinch you and make your ex - trem - i - ties numb.

Tempo I

I do mir - a - cles, you want some curves.

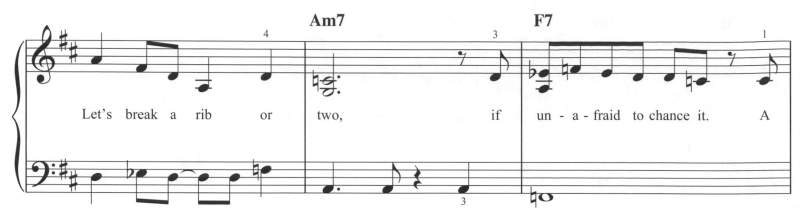

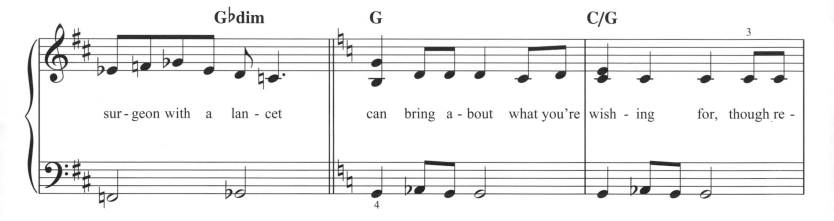

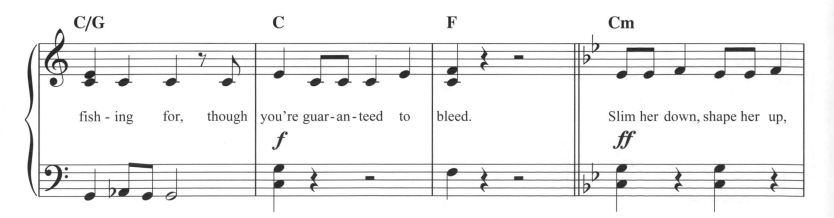

beau - ty has a cost. We may need to tape her up, but not all is lost.

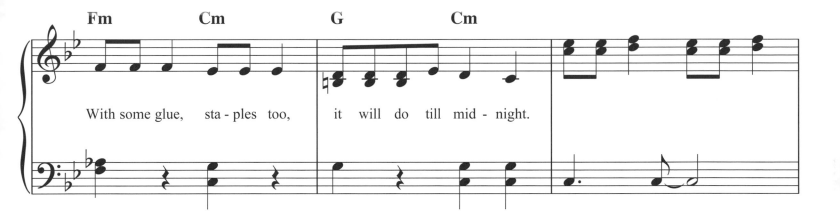

With some glue, sta - ples too, it will do till mid - night.

Let's skip sur-ger - y, we have-n't time. I tried some-thing less ex -

mf

treme, but come a lit - tle near - er and look in - to the mir - ror.

This I be - lieve's what you're wish - ing for. Who's that rav - ish - ing,

poco rall.

head - turn - ing girl that I don't rec - og - nize? And can it real - ly be that

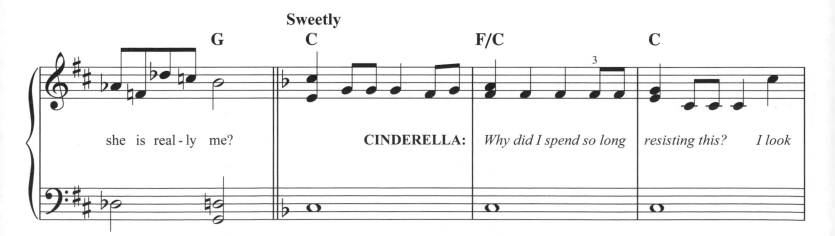

she is real - ly me? **CINDERELLA:** *Why did I spend so long resisting this? I look*

so much better! | GODMOTHER: Now. Put these shoes on. | They're made of solid crystal, | so... don't be surprised

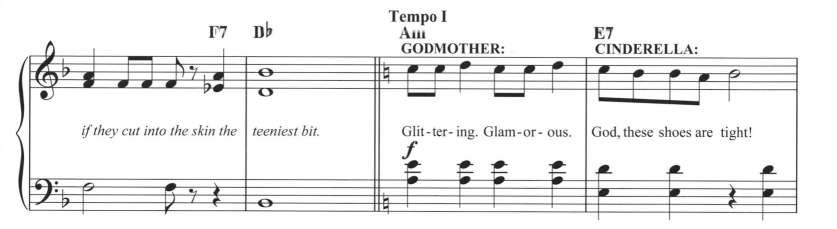

if they cut into the skin the | teeniest bit. | GODMOTHER: Glit-ter-ing. Glam-or-ous. | CINDERELLA: God, these shoes are tight!

GODMOTHER: He'll be feel-ing am-or-ous, | spell-bound at first sight. | CINDERELLA: I'm so fine, it's a sign,

he'll be mine by mid-night. | GODMOTHER: But, my pet, don't for-get | beau-ty has a price.

You will be in ag-on-y, let me be pre-cise. In this frock, by twelve o'-clock

you will be in tor-ment. Go a-head, knock him dead. Just be home by mid-night.
rall.

CINDERELLA:

Moderately, in 2

Look at me, Cin-der-el-la, I'm on fire af-ter
be Cin-der-el-la will be belle of the

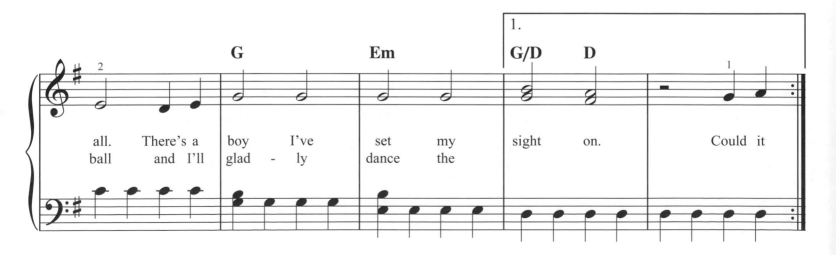

all. There's a boy I've set my sight on. Could it
ball and I'll glad-ly dance the

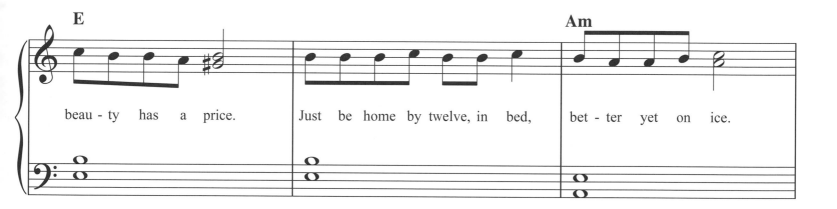

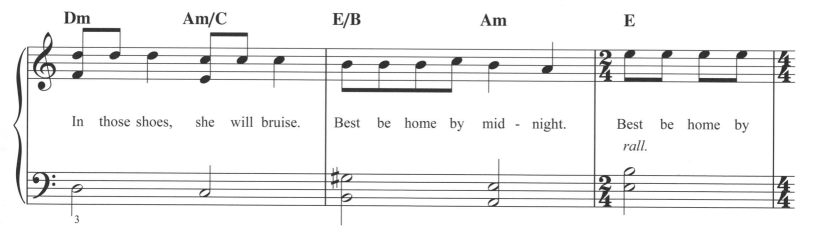

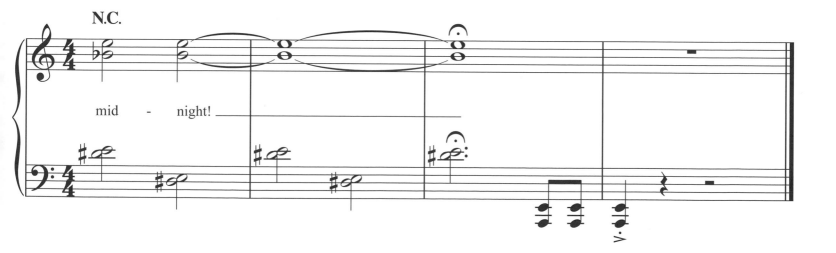

MOMENT OF TRIUMPH

Music by ANDREW LLOYD WEBBER
Lyrics by DAVID ZIPPEL
Book by EMERALD FENNELL

Brightly

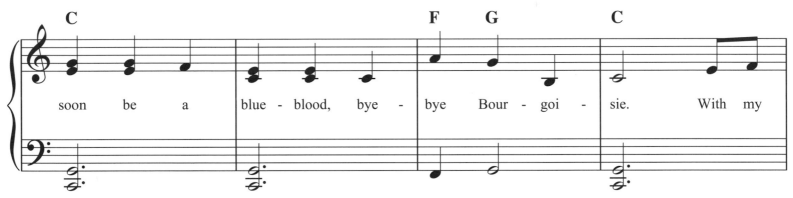

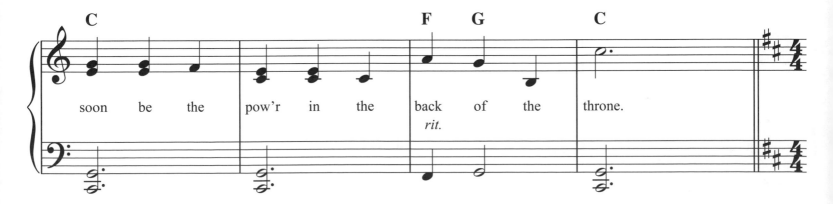

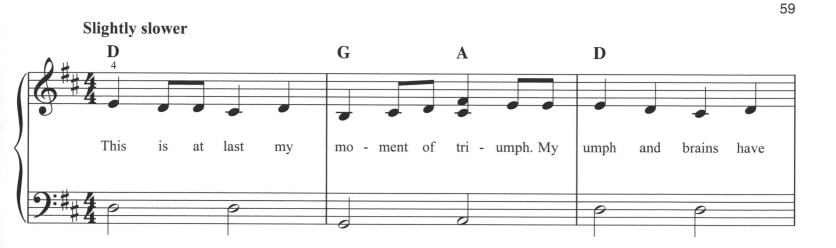

Slightly slower

This is at last my moment of tri-umph. My umph and brains have

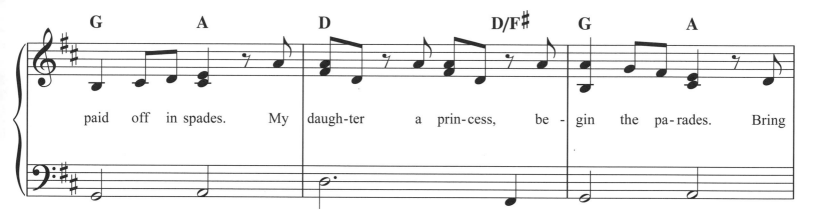

paid off in spades. My daugh-ter a prin-cess, be-gin the pa-rades. Bring

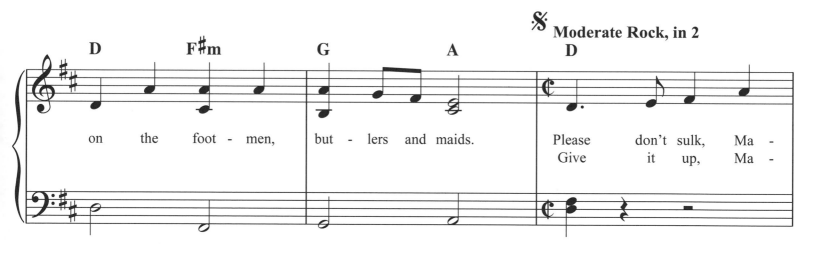

Moderate Rock, in 2

on the foot-men, but-lers and maids.

Please don't sulk, Ma-
Give it up, Ma-

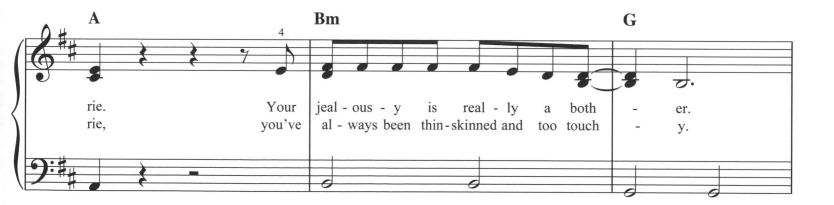

rie.   Your jeal-ous-y is real-ly a both - er.
rie,   you've al-ways been thin-skinned and too touch - y.

D   A   Bm

You   were run - ner - up.   Some - | day we'll raise a cup at your nup -
Now   the se - cret's   out   that | I pre - fer A - dele, but you al -

G   D   A

- tial day.   You're | not   my cup   of | tea.   The
- ways knew.   We'll | find you some | duke   so

C   G   D   A

truth is I de - test - ed your fa - ther. | He was a bore, —
you can lord it o - ver some duch - y. | But for to - day, —

To Coda ⊕
Slowly, freely

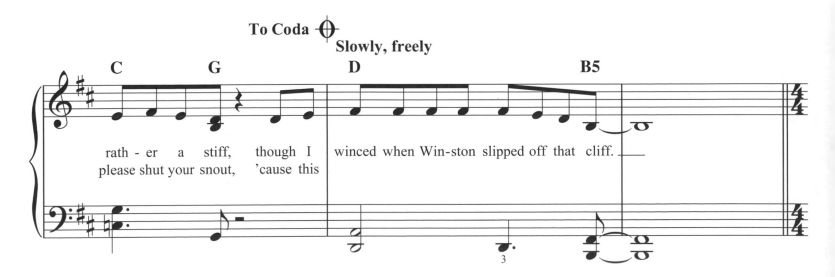

C   G   D   B5

rath - er a stiff, though I | winced when Win-ston slipped off that cliff. —
please shut your snout,   'cause this

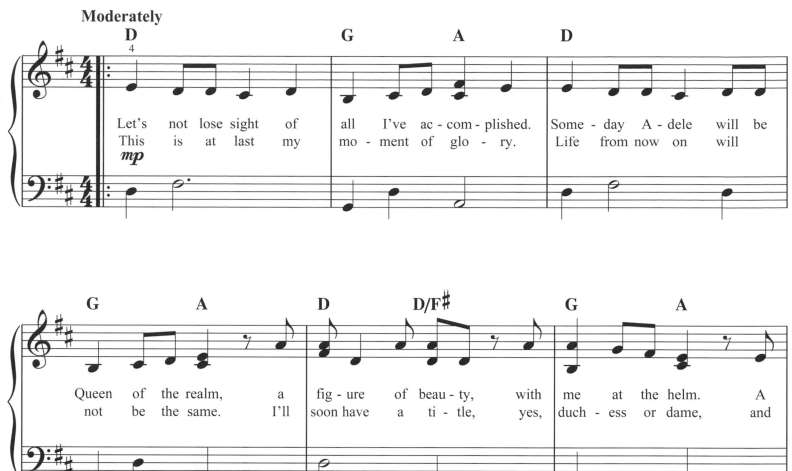

Moderately

Let's not lose sight of all I've ac-com-plished. Some-day A-dele will be
This is at last my mo-ment of glo-ry. Life from now on will

Queen of the realm, a fig-ure of beau-ty, with me at the helm. A
not be the same. I'll soon have a ti-tle, yes, duch-ess or dame, and

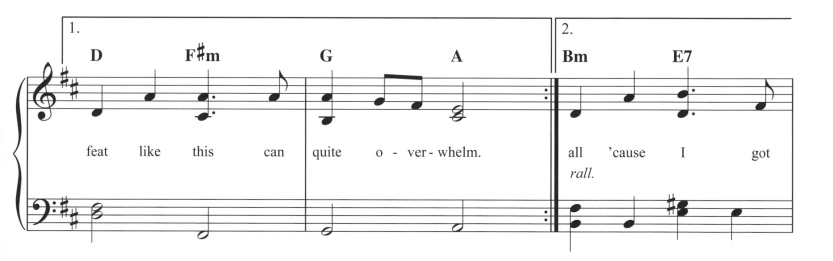

1.
feat like this can quite o-ver-whelm.

2.
all 'cause I got

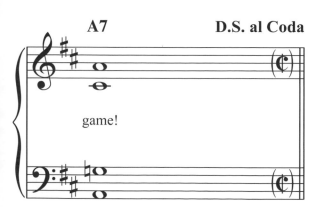

A7   **D.S. al Coda**

game!

CODA   **D**

wed-ding day is all a-bout me.

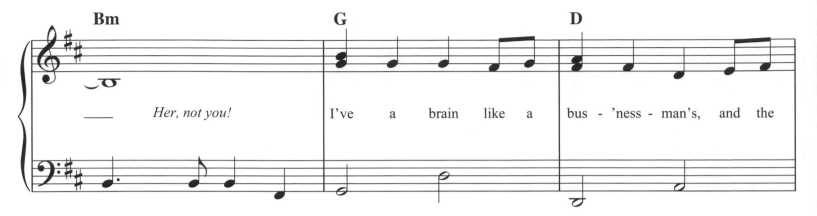

Her, not you! I've a brain like a bus - 'ness - man's, and the

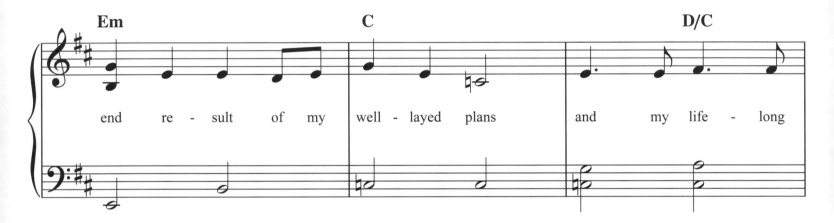

end re - sult of my well - layed plans and my life - long

schemes brought to pass my dreams.

MARIE:
Un - fair, un - kind, un - loved,

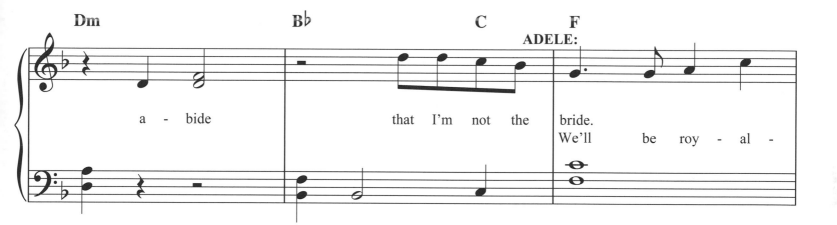

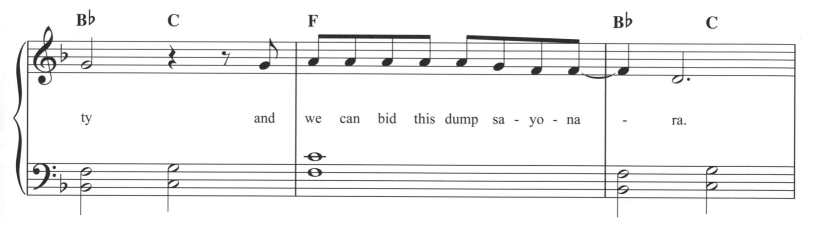

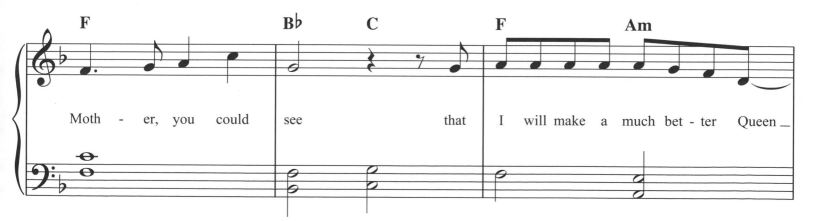

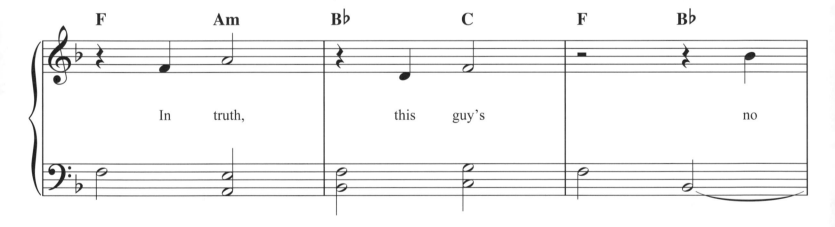

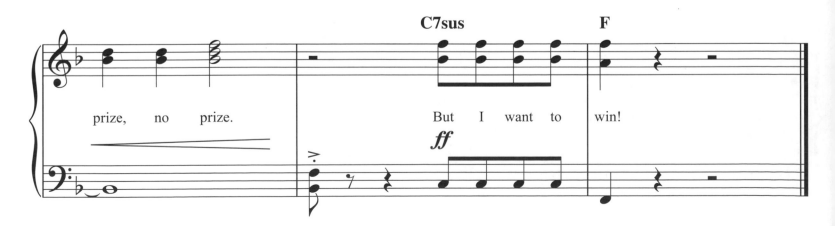

I KNOW I HAVE A HEART

Music by ANDREW LLOYD WEBBER
Lyrics by DAVID ZIPPEL
Book by EMERALD FENNELL

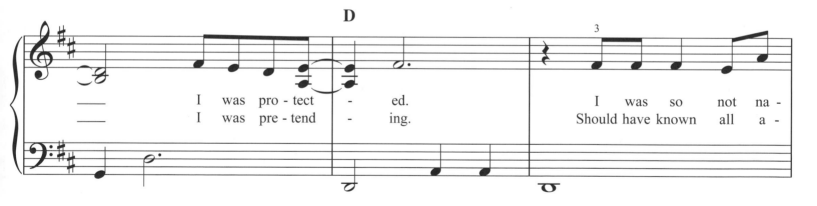

walked out be - fore _____ I was re - ject - ed.
girl who's like me _____ there's no hap - py end - ing.

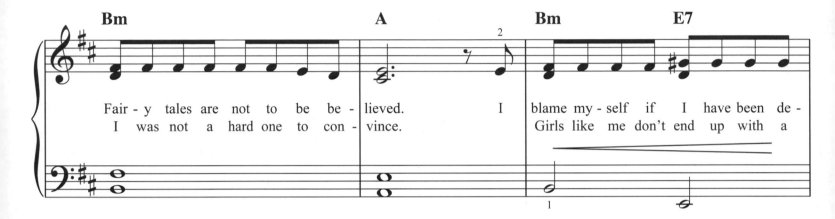

Fair - y tales are not to be be - lieved. I
I was not a hard one to con - vince. Girls like me don't end up with a

ceived. I was fine on my own.
prince. Found out love is a hoax,

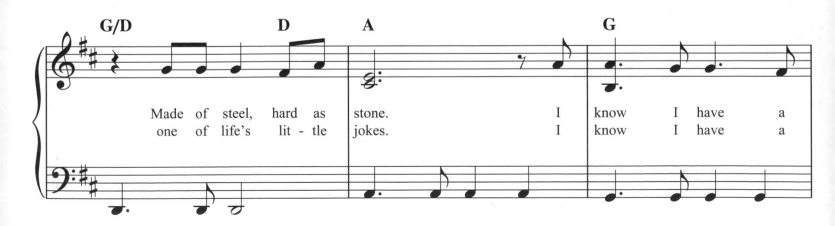

Made of steel, hard as stone. I know I have a
one of life's lit - tle jokes. I know I have a

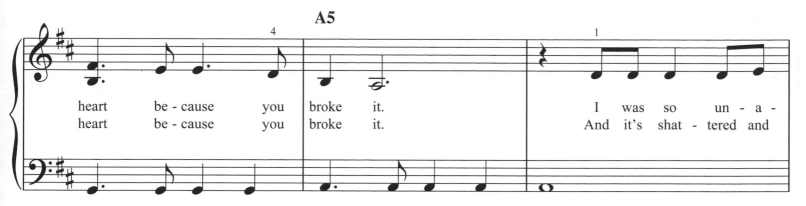

heart be - cause you broke it.
heart be - cause you broke it. And it's shat - tered and I was so un - a -

ware that I could fall so
bruised, and now the laugh's on

hard, but what good is a heart if you don't
me. An - y - one want a heart that's bare - ly
mp

care?
used?

Like a dam - sel in dis -

Fair - y tales are not to be be -
p

lieved. I blame my-self if I have been de - ceived.

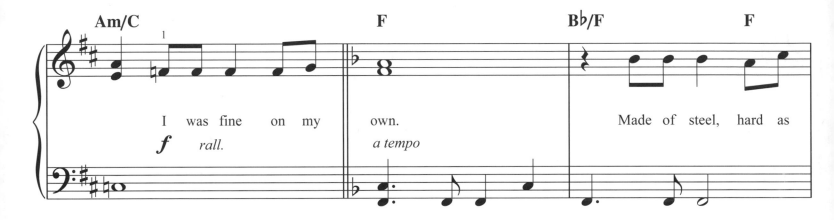

I was fine on my own. Made of steel, hard as

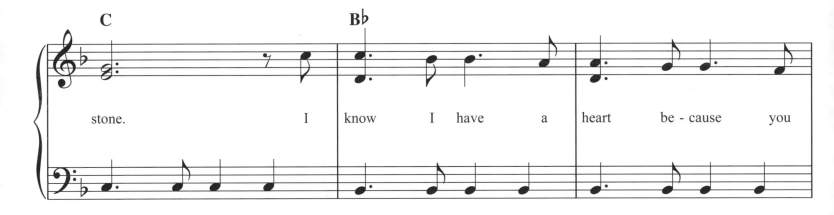

stone. I know I have a heart be-cause you

broke it. I was so un - a - ware

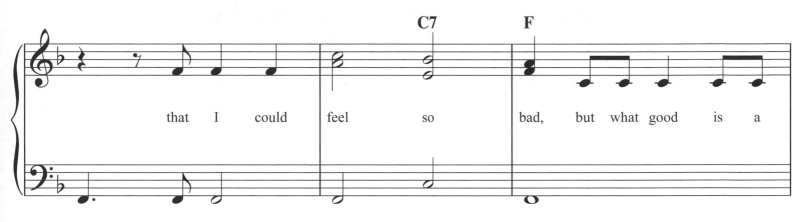

that I could feel so bad, but what good is a

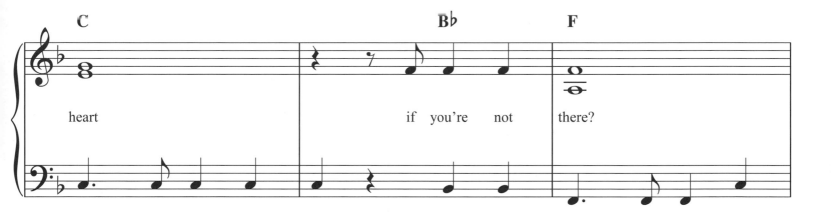

heart if you're not there?

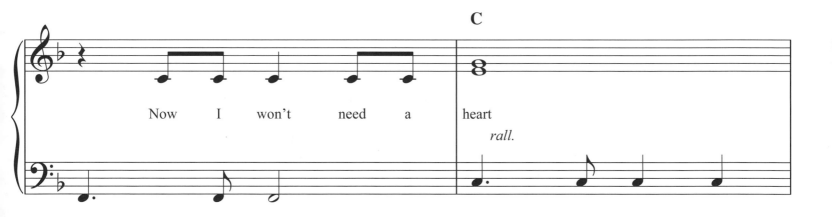

Now I won't need a heart

rall.

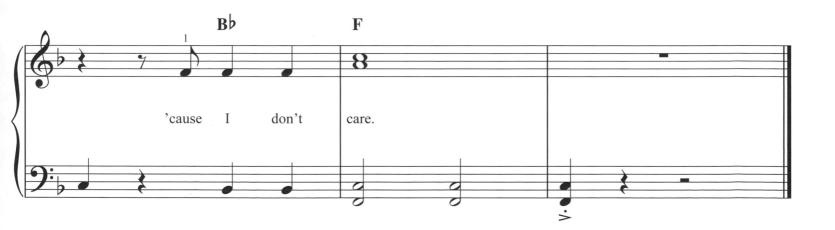

'cause I don't care.

I AM NO LONGER ME

Music by ANDREW LLOYD WEBBER
Lyrics by DAVID ZIPPEL
Book by EMERALD FENNELL

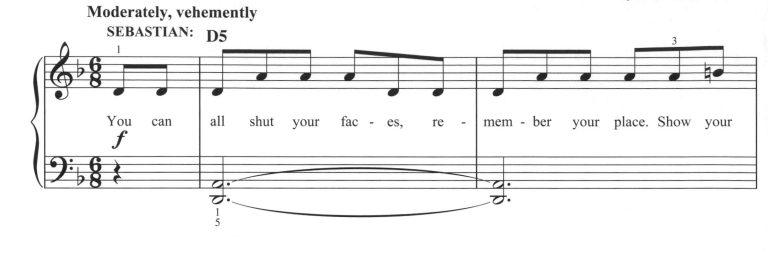

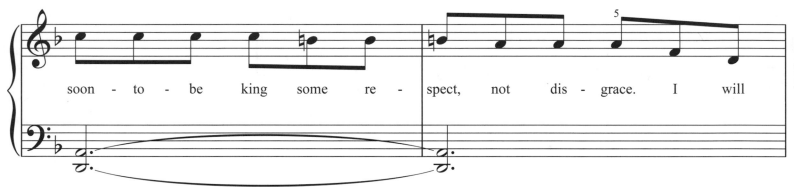

me. And I could be a ty-rant, you'll just wait and see. I am

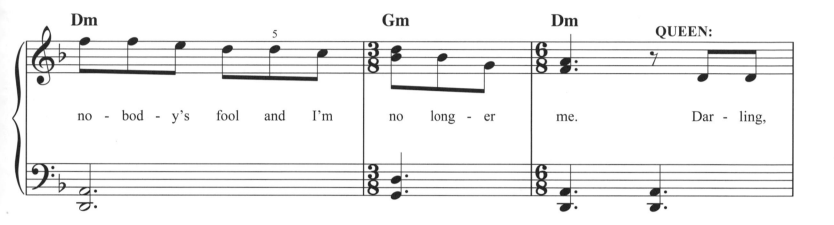

no-bod-y's fool and I'm no long-er me. Dar-ling,

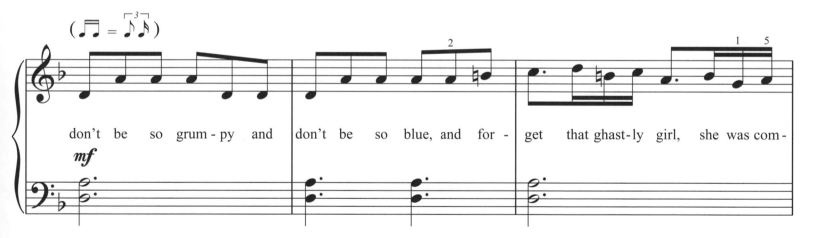

mf

don't be so grum-py and don't be so blue, and for-get that ghast-ly girl, she was com-

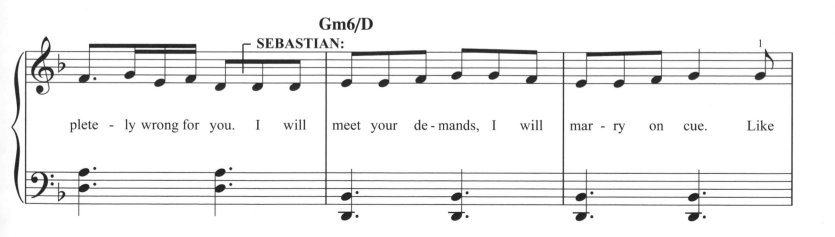

plete-ly wrong for you. I will meet your de-mands, I will mar-ry on cue. Like

you, I'll be cold and pas-sion-less too, 'cause I'm no long-er

(to the HUNKS):

me. You should grov-el and fawn or you'll all soon be gone. I can

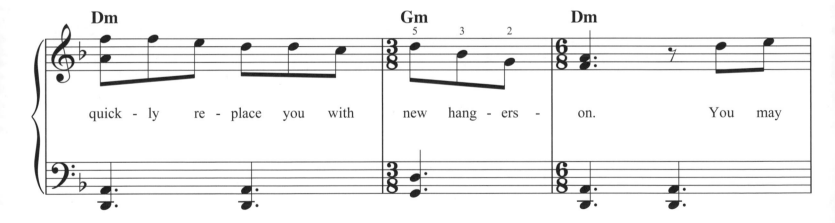

quick-ly re-place you with new hang-ers - on. You may

think me un-cool if I rule by de-cree. I'm the big dog in Belle-ville, but

maid. Sweet - ie, now you know it's all a show, a cyn - i - cal cha -

SEBASTIAN: **Dm**

rade. I will do as you ask, I will put on my mask and I'll

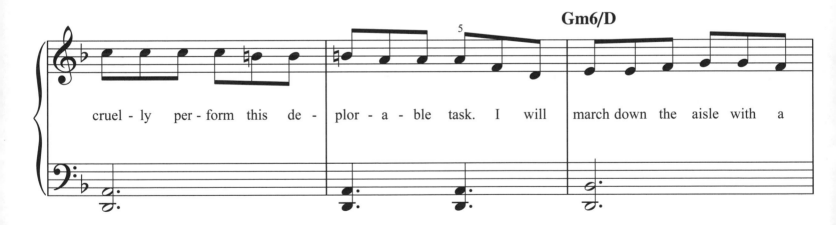

Gm6/D

cruel - ly per - form this de - plor - a - ble task. I will march down the aisle with a

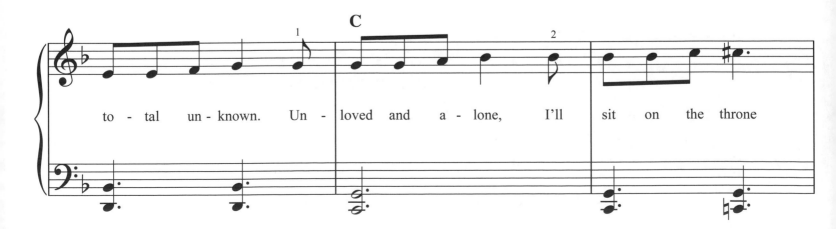

C

to - tal un - known. Un - loved and a - lone, I'll sit on the throne

as I'm no long - er me. And my soul will be crushed by the

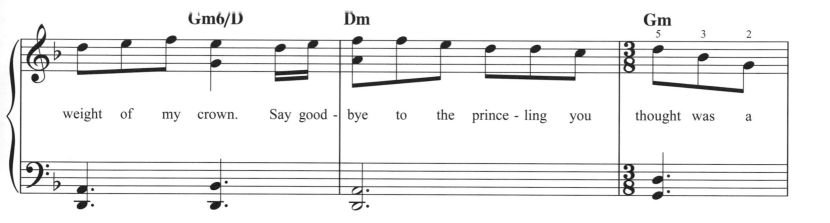

weight of my crown. Say good - bye to the prince - ling you thought was a

clown. So you all need - n't wor - ry, I'm no long - er me. For what's

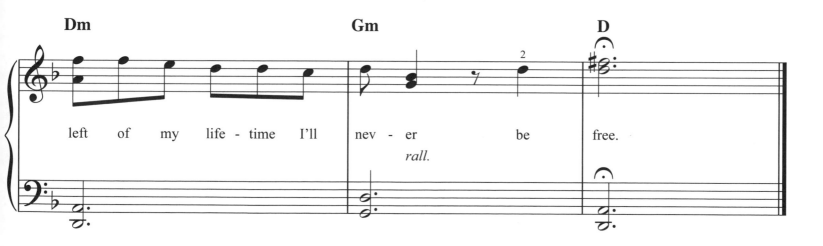

left of my life - time I'll nev - er be free.

THE WEDDING MARCH

Music by ANDREW LLOYD WEBBER
Lyrics by DAVID ZIPPEL
Book by EMERALD FENNELL

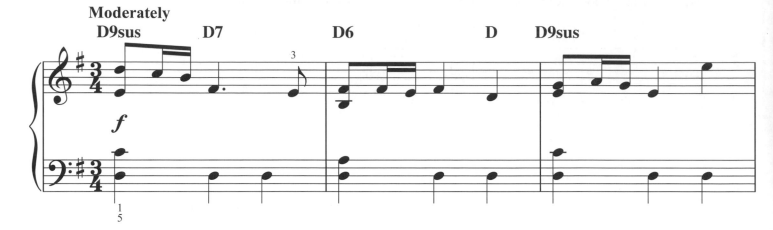

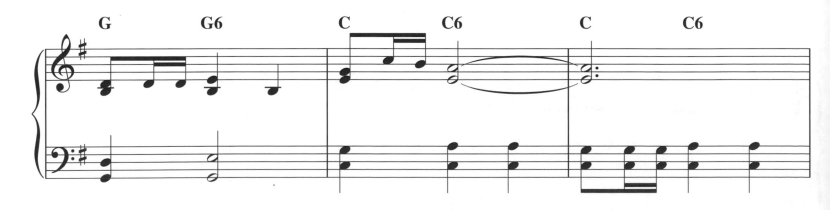

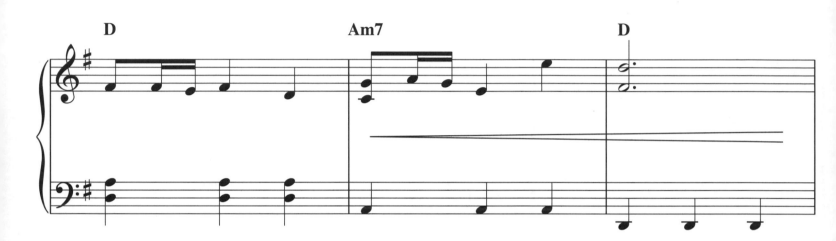

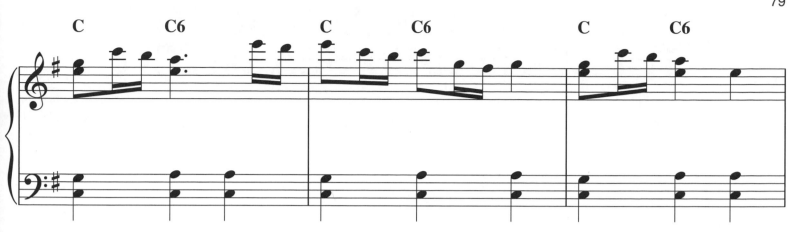

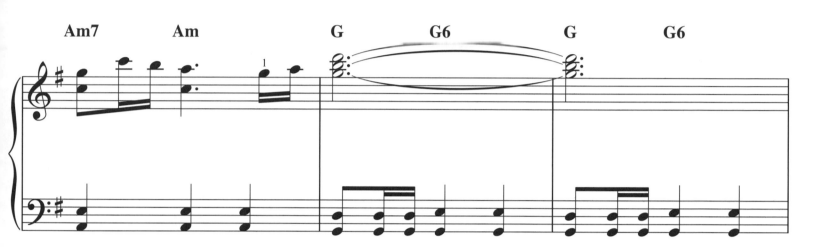

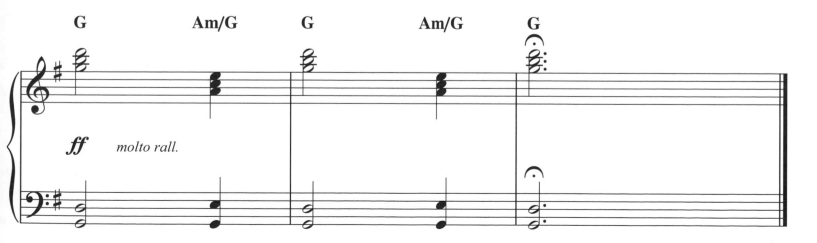

THE VANQUISHING OF THE THREE-HEADED SEA WITCH

Music by ANDREW LLOYD WEBBER
Lyrics by DAVID ZIPPEL
Book by EMERALD FENNELL

CHARMING: I could see the u-ni-verse was call-ing me to cut her down to size. *(Size!*

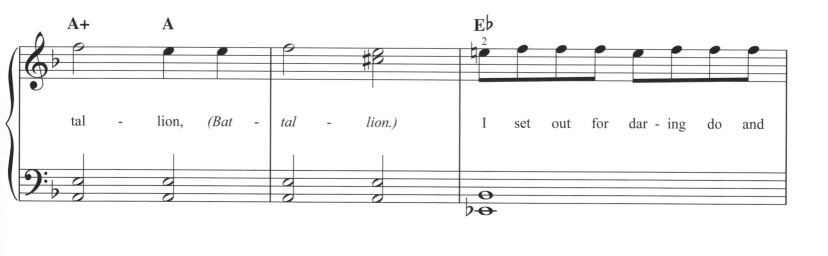

CHARMING: *Size! Size!)* All a-lone but strong as a bat-

tal - lion, *(Bat - tal - lion.)* I set out for dar-ing do and

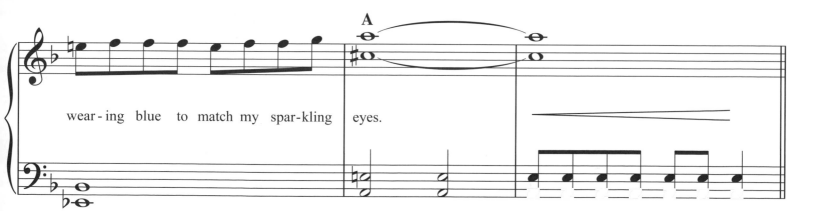

wear-ing blue to match my spar-kling eyes.

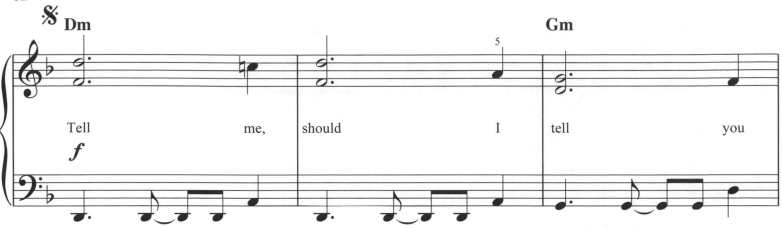

Tell me, should I tell you more? *(Yes!)*

Tell me I'm the daz - zling prince that you still a -

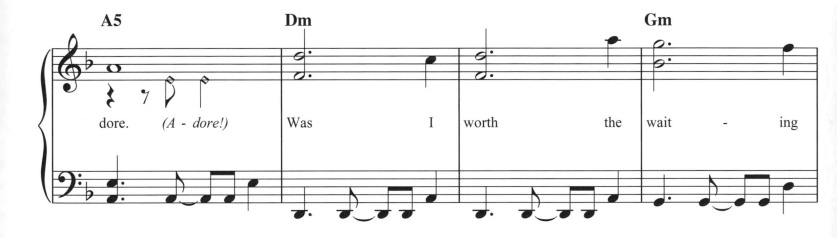

dore. *(A - dore!)* Was I worth the wait - ing

To Coda

for? *(Yes!)* Do you love me, did you miss me? Yes we love you, yes we miss you!

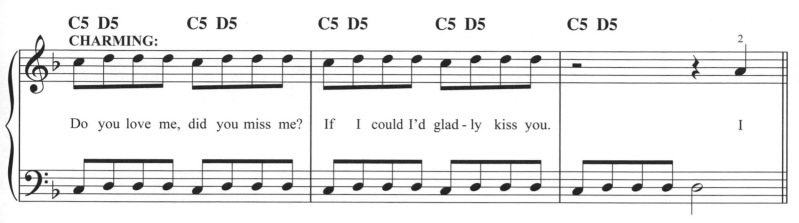

CHARMING:
Do you love me, did you miss me? If I could I'd glad-ly kiss you. I

knew once I'd found her I'd quick-ly sub-due her. A

shark of my ac-quain-tance said he'd lead me right to her.

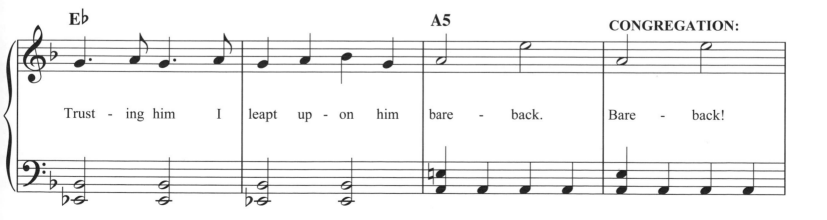

Trust-ing him I leapt up-on him bare-back. Bare-back!

CONGREGATION:

CHARMING:

We went rac-ing 'cross the seas and hur-tling t'ward her un-der-wa-ter cave.____

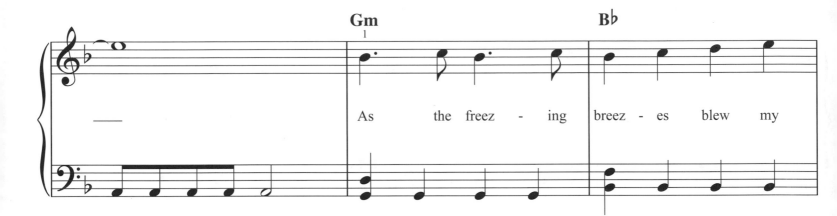

____ As the freez - ing breez - es blew my

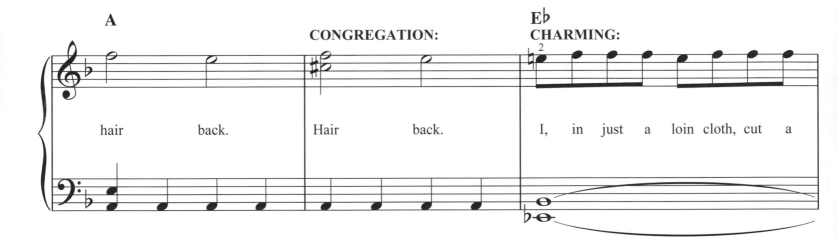

hair back. **CONGREGATION:** Hair back. **CHARMING:** I, in just a loin cloth, cut a

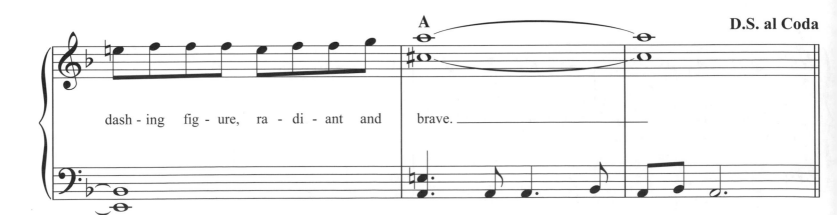

dash-ing fig - ure, ra - di - ant and brave.____

D.S. al Coda

CODA
CHARMING:

Do you love me, did you miss me? If I could I'd glad-ly kiss you.

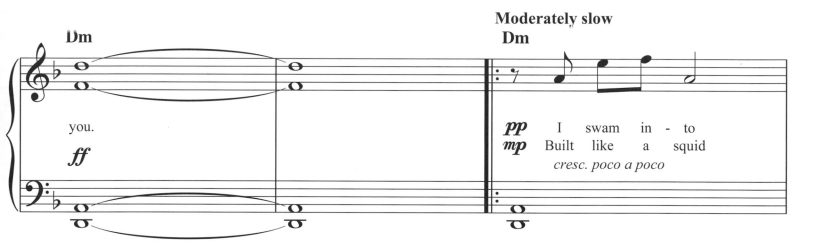

Moderately slow

pp I swam in-to
mp Built like a squid
cresc. poco a poco

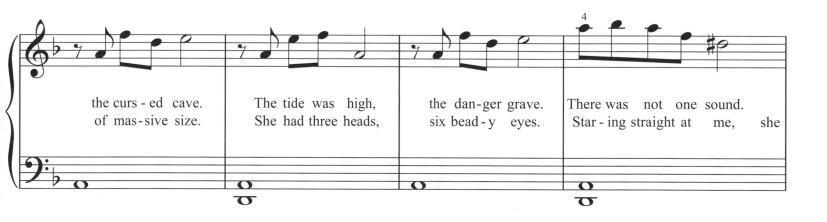

the curs-ed cave. The tide was high, the dan-ger grave. There was not one sound.
of mas-sive size. She had three heads, six bead-y eyes. Star-ing straight at me, she

It was dark and weird. Then the wi-ly witch ap- peared.
said to my sur-prise, "Shall we see who lives and dies?"

I slashed one head / to show who's boss. / The oth - er two
I heard a sweet / an - gel - ic sound. / Was I de - ceased?

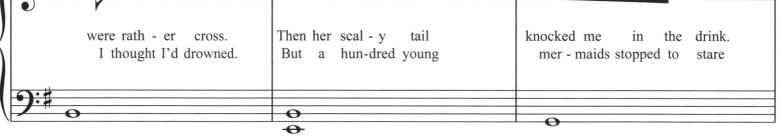

Db/G

were rath - er cross. / knocked me in the drink.
I thought I'd drowned. / But a hun-dred young / mer - maids stopped to stare

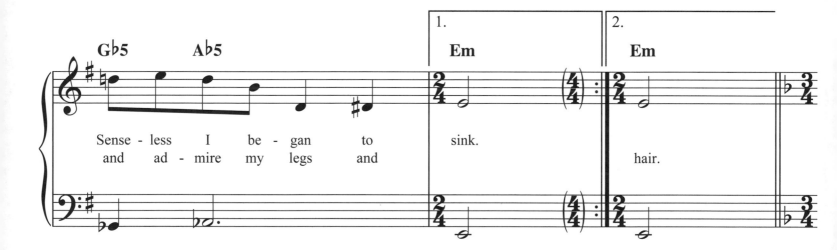

Gb5 **Ab5**

1. **Em**

2. **Em**

Sense - less I be - gan to / sink.
and ad - mire my legs and / hair.

Dm

They gave me air, / they saved my life. / They gave me back / my hunt-ing knife.

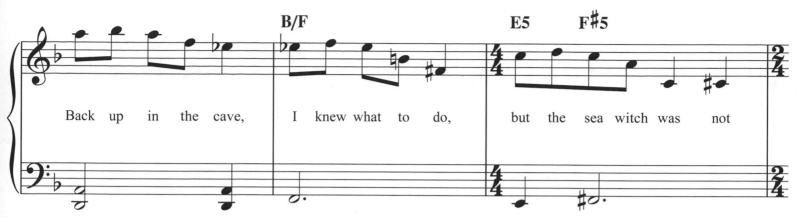

Back up in the cave, I knew what to do, but the sea witch was not

through. She caught me in her ten-ta-cles and knew she____

____ had got me where she want-ed me and an-y chance I'd shake her grip was

gone. When I was done five hun-dred pounds of

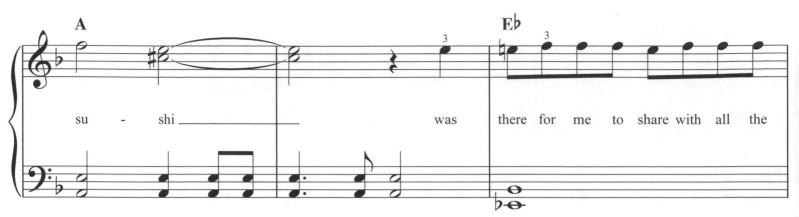

su - shi _____ was there for me to share with all the

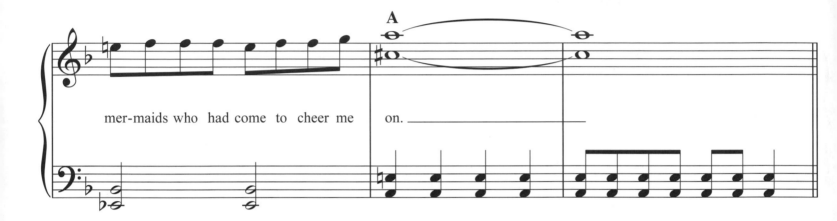

mer-maids who had come to cheer me on. _____

Tell me that you're glad I'm back. *(Yes!)*
Tell me, should I tell you more? *(More!)*

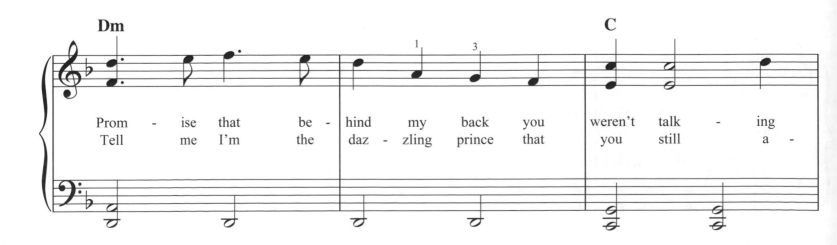

Prom - ise that be - hind my back you weren't talk - ing
Tell me I'm the daz - zling prince that you still a -

A   Dm

smack.   *(Yes!)*   Was   I   worth   the
dore.   *(Adore!)*

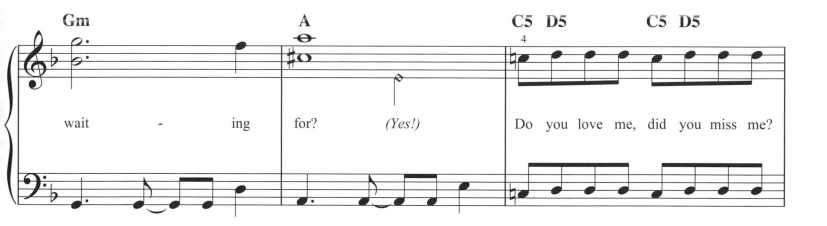

Gm   A   C5   D5   C5   D5

wait - ing   for?   *(Yes!)*   Do you love me, did you miss me?

C5   D5   C5   D5   C5   D5   C5   D5

CONGREGATION: **CHARMING:**

Yes we love you, yes we miss you!   Do you love me, did you miss me?

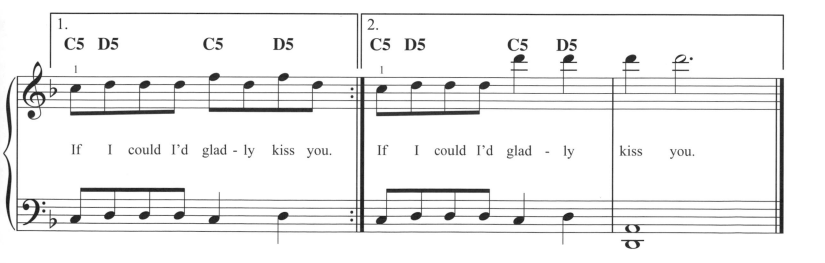

1.
C5   D5   C5   D5

If I could I'd glad - ly kiss you.

2.
C5   D5   C5   D5

If I could I'd glad - ly   kiss you.

FAR TOO LATE

Music by ANDREW LLOYD WEBBER
Lyrics by DAVID ZIPPEL
Book by EMERALD FENNELL

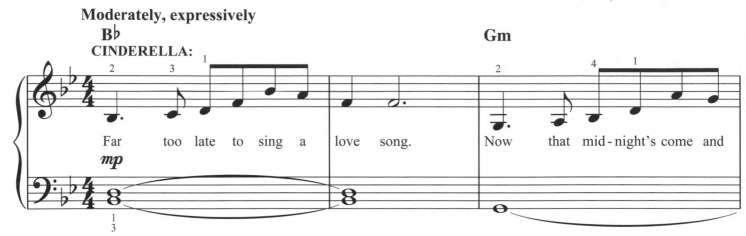

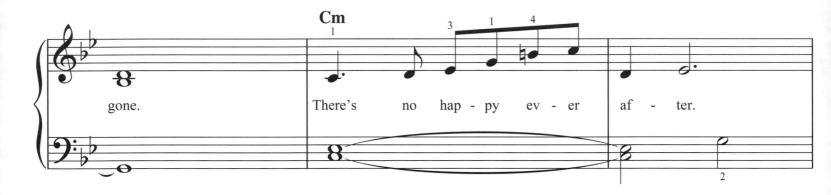

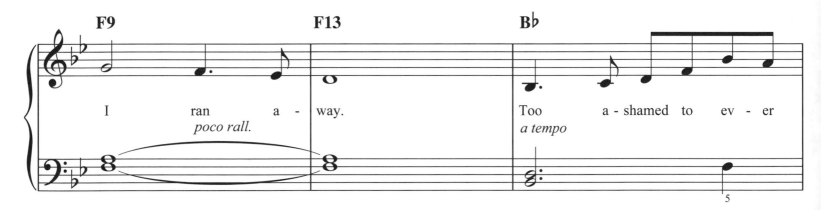

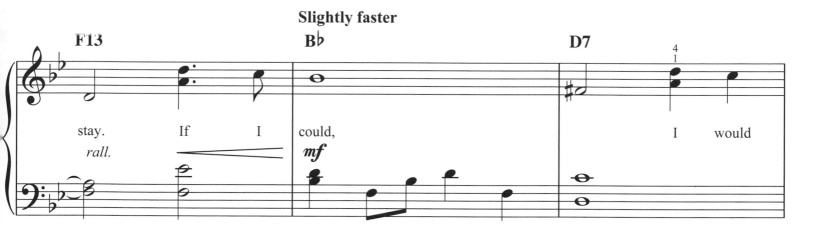

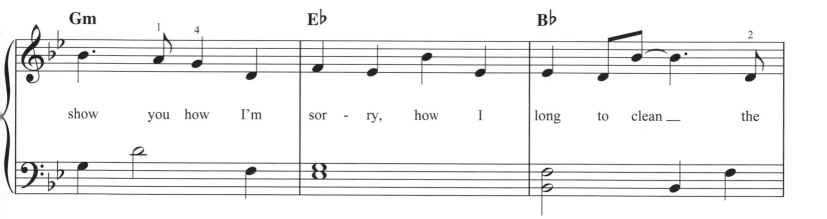

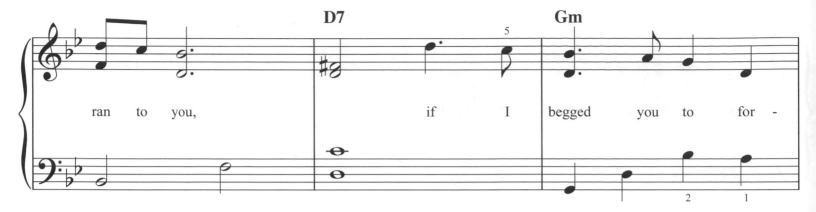

ran to you,   if I begged you to for -

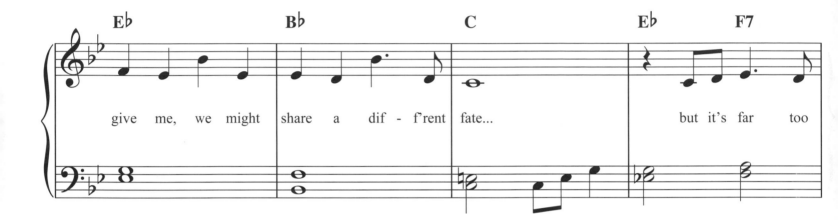

give me, we might share a dif - f'rent fate...   but it's far too

late. Far too late to sing a love song.

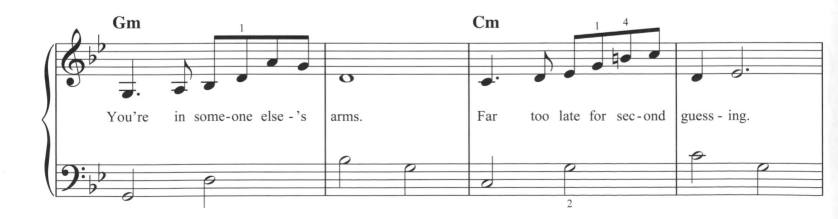

You're in some-one else -'s arms. Far too late for sec-ond guess - ing.

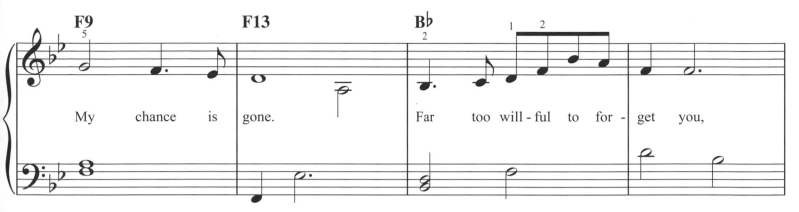

My chance is gone. Far too will-ful to for-get you,

though I have to let you go. There's no point in my ob-sess-ing.

Con moto

You're mov-ing on. If I could, I would

rall. *f*

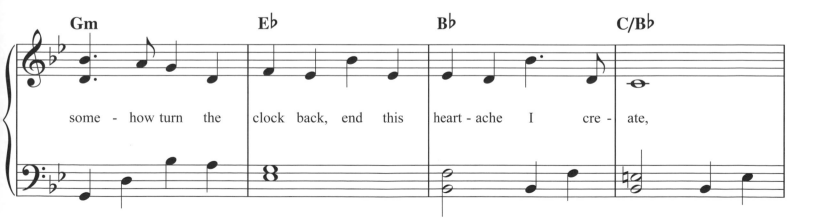

some - how turn the clock back, end this heart-ache I cre - ate,

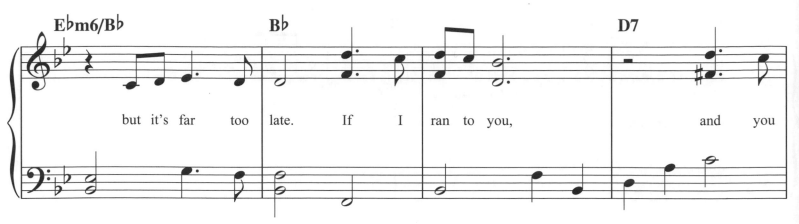

but it's far too late. If I ran to you, and you

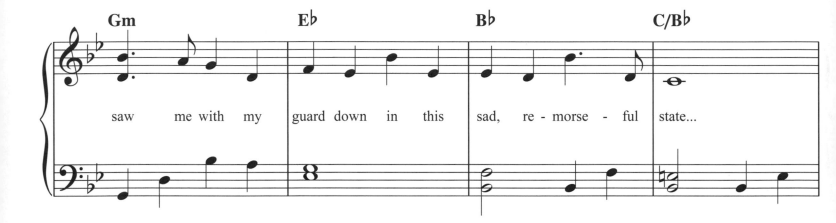

saw me with my guard down in this sad, re - morse - ful state...

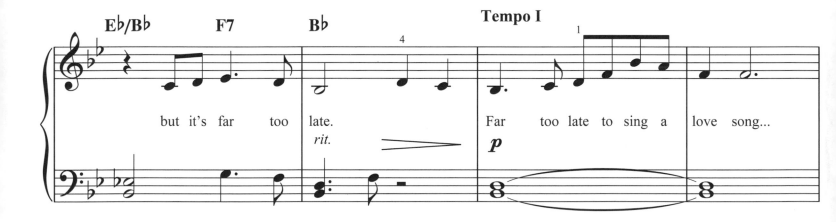

but it's far too late. Far too late to sing a love song...

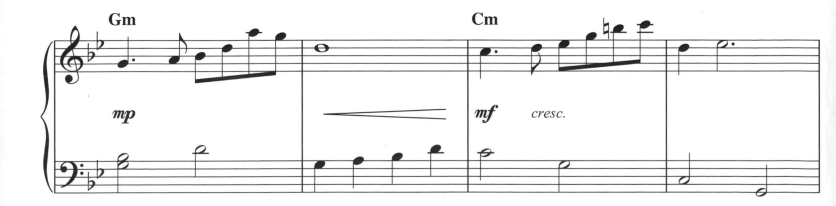

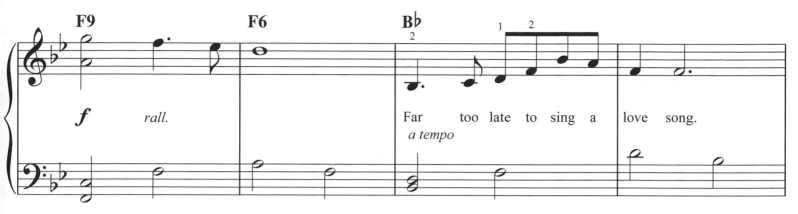

Far too late to sing a love song.

You're in some-one else -'s arms. Far too late for sec-ond guess - ing.

My chance is gone. If I could, I would

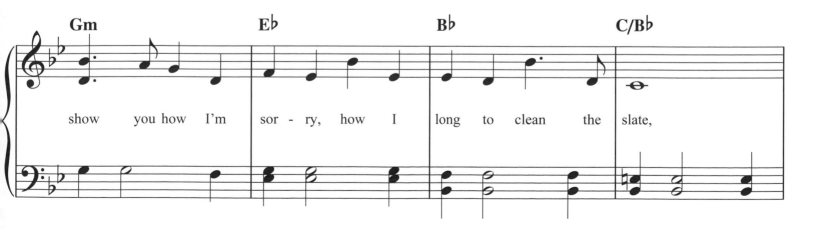

show you how I'm sor - ry, how I long to clean the slate,

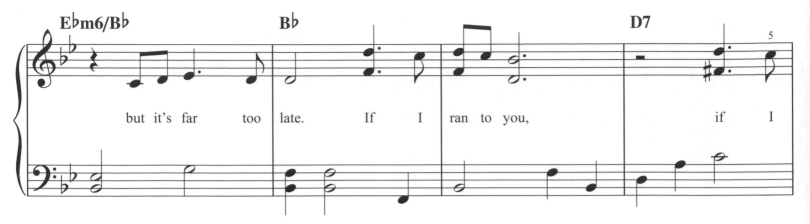

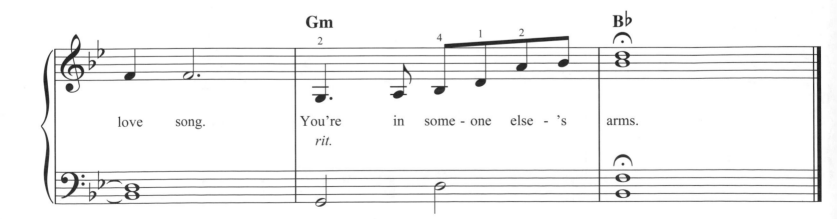